Transportation and the Disadvantaged

Transportation and the Disadvantaged

The Poor, the Young, the Elderly, the Handicapped

John C. Falcocchio
Edmund J. Cantilli
Polytechnic Institute of New York

Lexington Books
D.C. Heath and Company
Lexington, Massachusetts
Toronto London

Library of Congress Cataloging in Publication Data

Falcocchio, John C.
Transportation and the disadvantaged.

Includes bibliographical references.
1. Aged–United States–Transportation. 2. Physically handicapped–United States–Transportation. 3. Poor–United States–Transportation. 4. Youth–United States–Transportation. I. Cantilli, Edmund J., joint author. II. Title.
HE206.2.F3 388.4'0973 73-11648
ISBN 0-669-89557-1

Published simultaneously in Canada.

Printed in the United States of America.

International Standard Book Number: 0-669-89557-1

Library of Congress Catalog Card Number: 73-11648

Transportation is an agency by which every part of society is brought into relation with every other.

C.H. Cooley, 1894

Contents

List of Figures

List of Tables

Foreword

The importance of this work lies in the fact that it identifies a cluster of transportation problems encountered by certain ever-growing segments of American society, and it also points to some scientific methods for dealing with each of the problems identified. The problems are those of persons among us, who, for reasons peculiar only to them, are classified as the disadvantaged. The new approaches to solutions are based on available but widely scattered and diversified kinds of information and statistical methods. The authors have very realistically and cleverly assembled, and made relevant, many differing but related engineering concepts into a guide which will be of great value to the transportation policy maker, design engineer and operator.

The problems of the poor, the young, the elderly and the handicapped must eventually be dealt with before we as a nation concerned with the rights and freedoms of people will have achieved that often-mentioned greatness as a free society. The poor in the central cities and rural areas of the states cannot get to places of possible employment because of inadequate low-cost public transportation. Many of the nation's young people are school drop-outs in communities which do not have low-cost adequate public transportation nor student fare subsidies. Many persons over sixty-five years of age refrain from using public transportation even when it is available due to fear of crowds, risk of injury upon boarding vehicles, lurching movements or physical violence. Most persons who are handicapped due to age, injury, congenital malfunction or for other reasons are unable, without special-design passenger facilities and equipment, to use mass transit services. All segments of our society, including the disadvantaged, need access to transportation which is safe, efficient, convenient, low-cost and free of physical, psychological and economic barriers.

Although it was nowhere stated in so few words, a freedom of mobility and accessibility for all people in our society seems intended in the Privileges and Immunities Clause of the Constitution. The early colonists brought with them the right to move about freely within and between and among the various British colonies in the New World. After the American Revolution, the former colonies were loosely united by the Articles of Confederation. A brief quotation from the Fourth Article embodies that freedom;

> To better secure and perpetuate mutual friendship and intercourse among the people . . . the people of each state shall have free ingress and regress to and from any other state, and shall enjoy therein all the privileges of trade and commerce. . . .

The framers of that policy must have envisioned the potential greatness of our nation and its vast variety of mobility needs. Subsequently and in their respective times, post roads, maritime commerce, canals, railroads, highways, airports and urban mass transit were subjects of that policy as it evolved. Today it is exemplified in a transportation network unequalled in the entire annals of mankind as to diversity of modes, quantity of facilities, volume and quality of services! One of its shortcomings however is that it extends an unequal privilege or an unequal freedom of mobility to the disadvantaged members of our citizenry.

This combined work of two transportation scholars addresses itself to an aspect of freedom, or lack of it, which is all too often avoided *in toto* or in part by transportation policy makers, planners, engineers, designers and operators. There are necessary social overtones implicit in this volume, in that it states in not so few words that the benefits which flow from accommodating the transportation needs of the disadvantaged cannot be evaluated in absolute returns on the capital investments. All people desire and should have the same general opportunities to pursue some gainful employment, to shop, to engage in recreational pursuits and to benefit from social interchange. Most persons classified among the disadvantaged are potential public transportation users and who could be great contributors to society and industry, given the freedom of mobility of the general populace.

Lloyd Peterson
Regional Representative of the Secretary
U.S. Department of Transportation

July, 1974
New York, N.Y.

Preface

This book is about the transportation problems faced by the disadvantaged: the poor, the young, the aged, and the handicapped. These groups are transportation-disadvantaged primarily because they number amongst them the greatest incidence of autoless individuals. Their transportation problems are identified and analyzed within the context of an automobile-oriented society.

The purpose of this book is to bring together the body of knowledge relative to the transportation problems of the disadvantaged. The consequences of a lack of transportation are examined relative to their effects on the groups affected. Transportation improvements are evaluated in terms of measurable impacts on specific goals and planning objectives. For the poor, an analytical model has been developed which permits the evaluation of economic benefits and costs of transportation improvements for an important component of this segment of the population. Current transportation planning methodology and criteria are reviewed and recommendations for improving the transportation planning process at the local level are provided.

The material assembled to write this book comes from a wide range of sources, and represents typical examples of problems and solutions attempted in many areas of the United States. This book presents the issues of transportation problems of the disadvantaged in a manner which makes the material of interest to the general public and useful to the professional interested in planning and transportation.

Acknowledgments

The authors wish to acknowledge the assistance of many individuals who have helped with the data necessary for this book. A special debt is owed to Dr. Louis J. Pignataro, whose pioneering efforts in this area of transportation concern have provided us with the impetus and the inspiration to write this book.

Our thanks to Dr. William R. McShane for his contribution to the development of portions of this work, and to the U.S. Urban Mass Transportation Administration for sponsoring portions of the research described.

Finally, we wish to thank Mrs. Marion Fischetti who was ever so helpful in getting the final manuscript typed.

The authors assume responsibility for any errors of fact and judgment.

1 Background

The Problem

Those groups in the general population which do not partake of the "average" characteristics of that population, whether in terms of income, or physical capability, or mental maturity, may be termed "disadvantaged." The U.S. Department of Labor has had a definition of "disadvantaged," which follows:

An individual is described as *disadvantaged* if he is a poor person who does not have suitable employment and is (1) a school dropout, (2) a minority member, (3) under 22 years of age, (4) more than 45, or (5) handicapped.[1]

We will not go so far (or be so restrictive) as the Department of Labor. A closer approximation to our view here is found in the *1972 National Transportation Report,*[2] in which it is noted that

The segment of the nation's population that most critically needs basic community services is the same segment that tends to have the least physical access to these services. The young, the elderly, the poor, the handicapped, and the chronically unemployed should be able to take full advantage of free or low-cost health care services, welfare services, educational opportunities, banking and legal services, as well as recreational and social activities; but, their access to these opportunities is hampered by the following:

- They cannot afford or are unable to drive an automobile.
- They cannot afford public transportation.
- They reside in areas poorly served by public transportation.
- The design and service features of public transportation systems pose difficult health, maneuverability, or orientation problems for them.[3]

John Crain developed a slightly different terminology, with essentially the same definition. His "transit dependent" group includes the young, the poor and structurally unemployed, older persons, physically handicapped, and the carless members of suburban families where mass transit is nonexistent.

But "transit-dependent" or disadvantaged, the group with which we concern ourselves have lost certain rights, privileges or advantages available to the vast majority of citizens. The "advantages" which they are in some way denied include the freedom of mobility which is a characteristic of people of advanced nations throughout the world. That mobility can be translated, in one respect, as freedom of choice among the transportation modes. From another standpoint, mobility involves the capability to move about using *any* transportation mode, and from this standpoint, public transportation facilities are proving themselves inadequate for those groups in the general population who have the fewest choices among modes, and who, in fact, can be considered public transit-dependent.

A "problem" exists in transportation for the disadvantaged in that the available modes of transportation: auto, taxi, bus, train, airplane, are not available to these groups in one way or another. That way may be through *cost*, through *design* inadequacies, or through *operational* problems.

Cost will affect the travel habits and capability of those who find fares excessive: the *poor. Design* inadequacies will affect those who find it difficult to get on or off a public conveyance, or to be comfortable once on board: the *aged* and the *handicapped. Operational* deficiencies will affect those who lack knowledge of a system; those who find it difficult to reach the system; and those who find that motion characteristics of the conveyance make it difficult to use: the *young*, the *old*, the *handicapped.*

Since the old are to a great degree among the *poor*, while at the same time their failing powers place them among the *handicapped*, they become a major part of the problem. The *young*, excluding the handicapped young, become part of the disadvantaged in relation to transportation in that they may be too young to drive while at an age when they do not have the money easily available for public transportation.

But each of the categories of the "disadvantaged" is related to the others. If we define the "poor" as being those individuals with incomes under $4,275; the "young" as those under 17 years of age; the "old" as those over 65; and the "handicapped" as any person with mobility restrictions, then Figure 1-1 can be used to indicate how these groups represent the "outsiders" or "fringe" members of society. If a box is drawn whose dimensions are the age of 18 at one side and the age of 64 at another; the limit of "normal" physical motor and mental comprehension capability at a third; and an "adequate" income at the fourth, then the areas beyond the lines drawn are the "outsiders," the disadvantaged.

From another standpoint we can represent, as in Figure 1-2, the *poor* as one group which is transportation-disadvantaged, and the *handicapped* as another. The *young* and the *old* are not then disadvantaged due to their age, but only as they become part of one group (the poor) *or* the other (the handicapped) *or* both. With the young, the *very* young are in a sense handicapped, since the transportation system is either too complex for their individual use of it, or the steps are too high, etc. The older young can become part of the poor if their funds are inadequate.

With the aged, it is not age alone which creates a disadvantage, but restricted physical capability (a handicap) or reduced financial circumstance (poverty). It

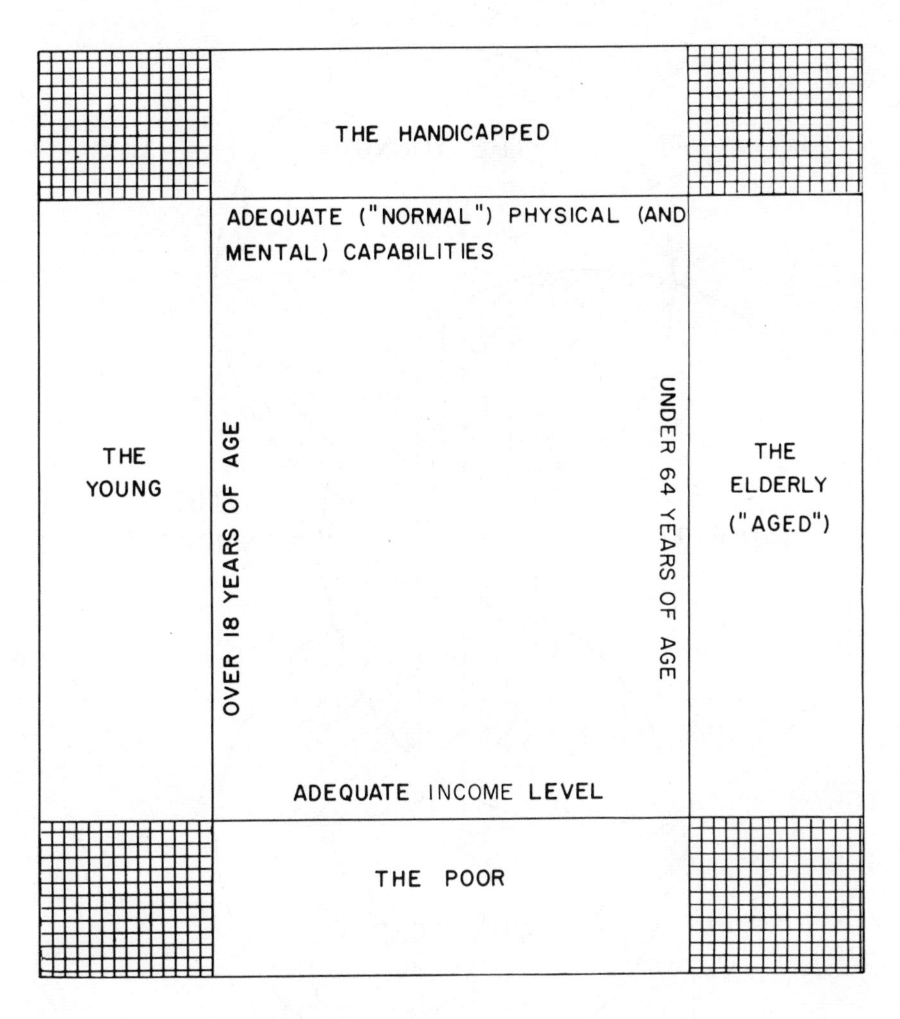

Figure 1-1. The Universe of Transportation Users

is with the aged, in fact, that we see most often the combination of being *poor* and *handicapped.*

This last illustration (Figure 1-2) can show how all the groups are interrelated. The young may have no other disadvantage, or they may be young *and* handicapped, or young *and* poor, or young, handicapped, and poor. The *handicapped* may also be young, *or* they may also be aged, *or* they may also be poor; they may also be handicapped, young, *and* poor, or handicapped, old, *and* poor. The *aged* may also be handicapped or poor, or both; the *poor* may also be young, or handicapped, or both, or they may be old, or handicapped, or both.

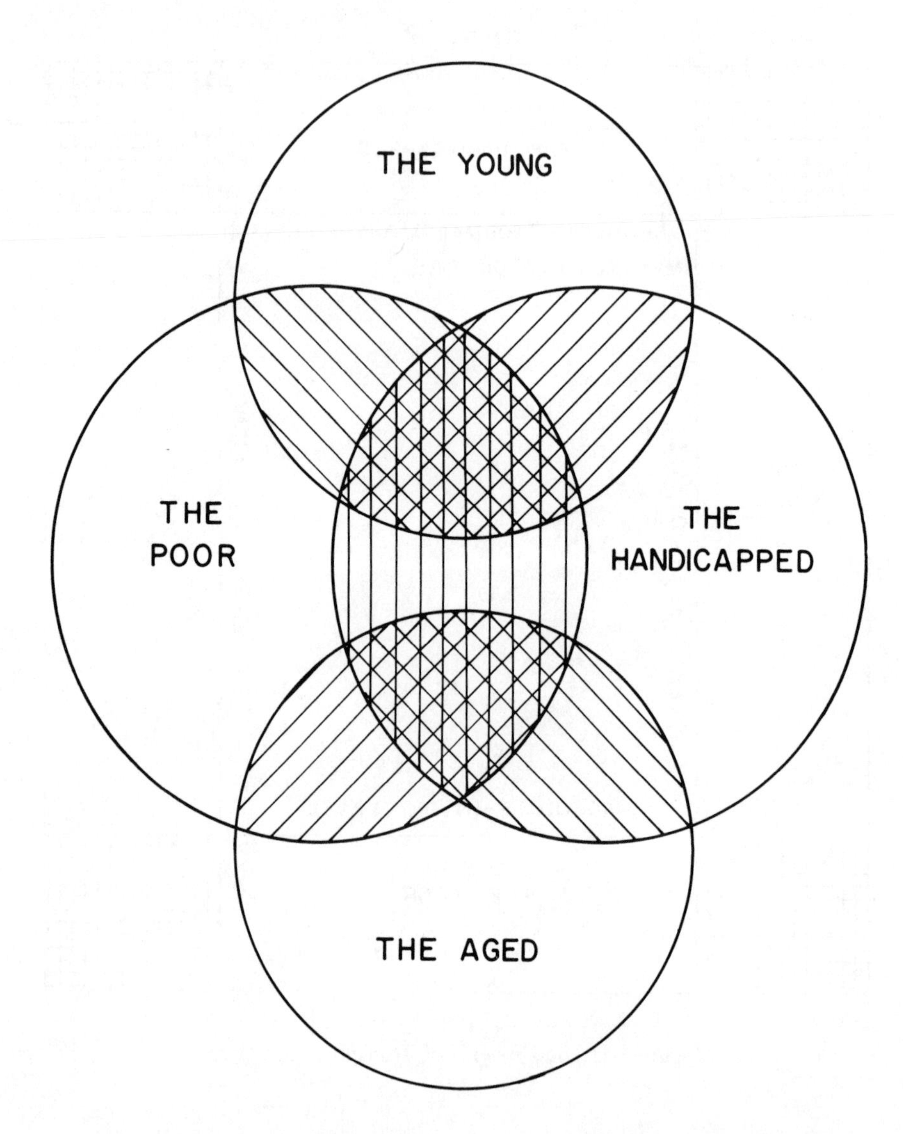

Figure 1-2. Overlap of Transit-Dependent or Transportation Disadvantaged

In sum it is a problem defined by two handicaps: money or physical (mental handicaps can be considered under the broad classification here of "physical") restrictions.

The Importance of the Problem

The poor, the young, the aged, and the handicapped may constitute anywhere from 25 to 50 percent of the population of the United States.[4] The extent of the "transit-dependent" or "disadvantaged" depends upon definition. In three of the categories, at least, the extent of that population can be legislated, or defined arbitrarily. In the fourth category, the handicapped, there remains an element of arbitrary definition, but the real difficulty is in identification. Estimates of the population of handicapped vary a great deal, even among experts in the field.

But the "importance of the problem" can be measured in ways other than by numbers or percentages of other numbers. The poor, the young, the aged, and the handicapped represent those members of the population who are at the fringes of the total population, in one way or another. The *poor* do not partake of the ability most people have for free decision in transportation matters. Not totally free, by any means, for even the most affluent of the affluent society, but most middle class workers and their families have that choice of auto or mass transit (if it exists at all), or mass transit or taxicab (on occasion), or bus or train or airplane for longer distances.

The *handicapped* do not partake of that element of free decision from another aspect: can they *use* the conveyance at all (or is the conveyance built, or equipped, for their use of it)? The *aged* are affected on both scores: their financial circumstances are reduced (and so they become part of the poverty group); and their physical capacities (to a great degree) become restricted, making them, if they are physically affected at all, part of the handicapped group. The *young* are considered disadvantaged, if at all, in that they are in a period of life in which they cannot be self-determinate in mode of transportation primarily due to lack of funds.

The Poor

Officially the "poor" in American society are recognized as those individuals earning less than $2,101 in a year. Depending on family size, this total (considering both farm and nonfarm families) can climb to $6,917 for a family of seven.

This means that, in 1972, 12 percent of the U.S. population was officially "poor."[5] This monetary handicap affects the poor, as concerns transportation, by limiting their capability of owning an automobile, on the one hand, or of utilizing public transportation, as fares increase, on the other. For instance, in New York City in 1969, 37 percent of families owned no automobile, while in the Central Brooklyn Model Cities Area, a "depressed", or "poverty" area, it was 73 percent of families for that same year. But New York is well served by mass transit. Los Angeles' car ownership (at the other end of the spectrum), was 83 percent in 1967, while the Watts district, a poverty area, had a car ownership of 42.1 percent (Willowbrook, a contiguous area, had an ownership rate of only 20.6 percent!).

As another example, the New York City transit fare was increased from 15 to 20 cents in July, 1966 (one in a long series of fare increases from the five-cent fare of the 1940s to the current 35-cent fare). As a result, transit riding declined 2.5 percent on the subways and about 10 percent on the buses. The effect was greatest, in fact, on the disadvantaged: rush-hour trips were affected least; week-day, off-peak, and Saturday trips were affected most (this is travel for shopping, social, and recreation); the decline was greatest among lower income groups; the decline among those who pay more than one fare for a trip was greater than the average for all rides.[6]

This has occurred, in a steady erosion, with every fare increase! Where have all the riders gone? Some may have switched to private autos, but many were those at or near poverty level, who decided it would no longer pay for them to earn a meager salary with the increase in fare, and found it a net advantage to go on public welfare! Some others are perhaps more easily identified. While peak hours continue to run at (or over) capacity, off-peak hours have deteriorated in service, to the point of scheduled trains as much as 30 minutes apart, and buses up to an hour apart. This *off-peak* period is the one which strikes the disadvantaged most heavily, since, at least for the young, the aged, and the handicapped, it is the *off-peak* hours which are most amenable to their use of public transit. For the poor, off-peak usage is for non-work-oriented trips, such as shopping and entertainment, and so increases in fares, and decreases in service, strike the capability of the disadvantaged groups for a normally active life.

Most of us still recall the ghetto riots which rocked several American cities from coast to coast in the mid-1960s. The major such tragedy occurred in the Watts area of Los Angeles in the summer of 1965.

The McCone Commission, in its report on the causes of the Los Angeles riots, concluded:

The most serious immediate problem that faces the Negro in our community is employment—securing and holding a job that provides him with the opportunity for livelihood, a chance to earn the means to support himself and his family, a dignity, and a reason to feel he is a member of our community in a true and very real sense.[7]

Among the many factors which were identified as contributing to the high role of unemployment of minority groups (lack of skills and discrimination being the primary causes), the Commission recognized that *inadequate and costly transportation* creates a significant barrier to the employment of the poor:

Our investigation has brought into clear focus the fact that inadequate and costly public transportation currently existing throughout the Los Angeles area seriously restricts the residents of the disadvantaged areas such as South Central Los Angeles. This lack of adequate transportation handicaps them in seeking and holding jobs, attending schools, shopping and in fulfilling other needs. It has had a major influence in creating a sense of isolation, with its resultant frustrations, among the residents of South Central Los Angeles, particularly the Watts area.[8]

This finding by the Commission, and its recommendation to improve public transit service to employment centers as a means to reduce the geographic isolation of minority neighborhoods, was followed immediately thereafter by a Federal (HUD)-sponsored demonstration program in East and South Central Los Angeles. This program was designed to test the hypothesis that *improved transit service from that area to inaccessible employment centers would be helpful in reducing the high unemployment rate* among low-income residents.

Following the Watts example, similar projects were undertaken in other areas of the country. Among these, the Long Island employment-transportation demonstration project[9] is a rather significant one.

In the past seven years several cities conducted studies to investigate the possible link between inadequate transportation and unemployment.[10] Available literature, however, gives no determination of the magnitude of cause-effect measures between transportation availability and employment. Such a deficiency was also stated by Ornati[11] in his study of New York City's low-income areas:

> Policies aimed at reducing employment-related poverty must respond to the self-evident fact that travel inconvenience is a barrier to employment. *The extent of this barrier is not known.* Nor has any estimate been made of the degree to which increasing the convenience of travel can reduce the employment-related poverty (p. 3).

The costs for conducting operational tests and experiments to demonstrate the feasibility of improving public transportation service to lower unemployment in low-income areas are high. Table 1-1 gives an example of how high they can be.[12]

The results produced by these projects did not, however, present a clear picture of the role of transportation in the low-income labor market. For example, *Floyd* stated: "that other factors may be more critical is apparent from the Los Angeles employment data which shows that of 9,383 project area residents who applied to the Department of Employment for jobs, 7,980 (85 percent) had not even been referred because they lacked the necessary skills."[13] Similar findings were reported for the Long Island project.[14]

Table 1-1
Demonstration Program Funding

Location	Federal Grant[a]
Los Angeles (East & South Central)	$2,700,000.
Long Island (Nassau & Suffolk Counties)	2,000,000.
St. Louis Metro Area	1,150,000.
Buffalo Metro Area	500,000.

[a]Usually 90 percent of total project costs are covered by the federal government.

Presumably, the availability of appropriate transport services linking low-income areas and employment centers is only *one* aspect of the complex problem associated with reducing the disparity between unemployment rates of ghetto residents and other parts of society. Another aspect is concerned with the broader issues of *motivating* and *assisting* the unemployed to take advantage of educational and training opportunities available to them. Perhaps the broad scope of the problem is best illustrated by the following statement:[15]

It is self-evident that the problems we are struggling with form a complicated chain of discrimination and lost opportunities. Employment is often dependent on education, education on neighborhood schools and housing, housing on income, and income on employment. We have learned by now the folly of looking for any single crucial link in the chain that binds the ghetto. All the links—poverty, lack of education, underemployment, and now discrimination in housing—must be attacked together.

Many proposed approaches to solving the poverty problem are long-range in nature. Reversing the trend of industry decentralization, reducing discrimination in housing, improved education and effective training programs, are all examples of possible solutions which are very much dependent on *time* for them to be effective. This is not to say that they are not appropriate measures. Rather, it is simply that they are not sufficient in offering *immediate* interim solutions. Transportation, therefore, appears to offer the only immediately applicable short-range answer. It is certainly not sufficient in *all* situations. But it is definitely necessary.

Further along in this book we will attempt to quantify the amount of transportation necessary to obtain an optimum contribution of this element to the reduction of unemployment. A brief review of the state of transportation technology is also presented. The discussion includes the problems brought about by the spread-city and the dispersal of job opportunities. The effect of widespread dependence on the automobile for mobility has left large numbers of transit-dependent users without adequate means of locomotion. Results of recent demonstration projects designed to improve employment opportunities for the poor and the mobility of the aged/handicapped are critically reviewed and evaluated for their effectiveness in meeting their intended objectives.

A discussion is presented, of the basic functions of transportation systems, as they relate to national, regional and local needs. The purpose of this discussion is to illustrate the issues which are relevant to the transportation-related problems of the disadvantaged. Emphasis is placed on the need to appraise the usefulness of a transportation system relative to its effect on the disadvantaged.

The variables which must be accounted for in analyzing the cause-and-effect relationship between transportation and the low-income worker are reviewed, considering the significance of transportation improvements as they concern the efforts of various institutions, both public and private, to cope with the problems of increasing employment opportunities for low-income workers. The characteristics of the low-income worker are discussed, as are factors other than transportation which may inhibit his employment status. These nontransportation causes are factored out for the purpose of isolating the effect of transportation. Then an employment-accessibility model is developed, calibrated, and evaluated using data from the Central Brooklyn Model Cities Area of New York.

In another chapter an example is developed for the purpose of illustrating the utility of the model in decision-making. Recommendations on how to use the model in other areas are outlined in the form of easy-to-follow guidelines which suggest a step-by-step procedure to planners and engineers working on similar problems.

A final section summarizes a proposed method for measuring the impact of transportation on the employment potentials of the low-income worker. It contains recommendations and caveats concerning the use of the method, and it suggests areas in which further research might be advisable to improve the effectiveness of the proposed method.

The Young

The young are a relatively ambiguous part of the so-called "disadvantaged," at least in the United States. While that portion of the population under eighteen is the country's greatest source of purchasing power for such items as 'pop' records, convenience foods, and motion pictures, it remains true that they can be considered "underprivileged" in deciding what mode of transportation to use, at least until the age of driver licensing (and auto availability) is reached. And in poverty areas and rural areas the problem of youth mobility is greatest.

As to one aspect of youth transportation, the young (under 18 years old, usually) are provided some kind of public transportation to go to and from school, usually at great effort and expense on the part of local governments. At the same time, however, during the school year 1971-72, in Indianapolis, 6000 high school students dropped out because they could not afford the bus fare to school.[16]

It is true, of course, that of all the "disadvantaged," the young perhaps have the greatest capability for self-help. Where the auto is unavailable, public transportation can at least physically be utilized. Where money is lacking for public transit, the young can walk long distances, cycle, or, ultimately, hitchhike. This last alternative is hardly available to the elderly, or to the handicapped. The poor could theoretically rely on begging rides, but we have not yet sunk to the levels of Depression-era freight-riding jobless. As noted in a government report, the young "are dependent upon others for private transportation. Otherwise, they walk, skate, bicycle, or hitchhike. All of these have inherent hazards, especially in congested urban areas."[17] As they grow older, the frustrations of transportation problems can "result in obsessive desire to obtain an automobile, regardless of its mechanical condition. This, of course, endangers their own safety as well as that of the general public."[18]

The recognition of a "problem" involving the young and transportation is of relatively recent vintage. With the category of the "young" it is possible to see the total remainder of the population reflected as "transportation-disadvantaged" at one time or another. Small children find it difficult to negotiate steps, to open doors, to use elevators or escalators: so do pregnant women, young women with small children, perfectly "average" men carrying large bags or packages, people with broken legs or other temporarily disabled, etc. In other words we can *all* become temporarily disadvantaged, and the category of "the young" would seem to represent a part of that temporary grouping.

In sum, while it is hard to think of the young as "disadvantaged," they certainly have important mobility problems, and these problems cannot be ignored.

In the remainder of this book we can look at means attempted at alleviating these disadvantages, and reasonable future alternatives.

The Aged

In 1970, 20 million persons were over the age of 65.[19] This is an arbitrary age for the classification of "aged," or "elderly." It represents "retirement age," but it suggests nothing of restrictions in eyesight, or hearing, or motor capabilities, which might relate to greater difficulty in using transportation. Many elderly citizens still drive their own automobiles. Such agility of mind and body excludes them from the "problem" group of the disadvantaged. Others have enough funds, friends, or interested relatives to take them where they wish to go when they wish to go. An estimate of the *handicapped* aged is 4 million.[20] These find it difficult, if not impossible, to lift themselves up bus steps; to grasp a handrail; to compensate for quick bus acceleration and turning movements; to hold themselves against sudden stops; to negotiate long flights of "subway" stairs; to find or comprehend bus stops and routings. Most of the aged are located in urban and suburban areas (see Table 1-2) but rural areas have a large segment.

The number of the aged is increasing; the *proportion* of the aged in the total population is increasing.

The general "problem" of the aged has grown in our public awareness perhaps since World War II. It has been a subject of popular interest, intermittently over the years, to discuss the phenomenon of greater and greater numbers of the elderly; of the creation of retirement areas and "villages"; and of the growing

Table 1-2
Elderly Population, 1970

Location	Total	Handicapped
Central city	6,600,000	1,300,000
Suburban	5,800,000	1,200,000
Rural	7,600,000	1,500,000
Total	20,000,000	4,000,000

Source: Manpower Report to the President, U.S. Department of Labor, transmitted to Congress, April 1971.

tendency of younger families to move away from or otherwise alienate themselves from parents and grandparents. A recent article in Time Magazine, for instance,[21] spoke of the "gradual devaluation of older people," as "one of the poignant trends of U.S. life," which is occurring at the same time that there is a spectacular growth in numbers of elderly persons. The elderly are more and more alienated from the younger elements of our welfare, and, treated like outsiders, they cluster together for mutual support.

About one-fifth of the elderly are employed. On the other hand, some five million of them are part of the "poverty" group, with an average income about half the income of people under 65 years of age.

Interest in transportation problems of the aged are of more recent vintage. Transportation problems have become of greater interest, if not importance, as greater concentrations of elderly have become apparent: as Florida became a retirement haven, and other towns and cities, such as East Orange, New Jersey, have found themselves with unusually large proportions of their population in the over-65 category. And these aged are major users of public transportation, especially for such purposes as shopping, visiting, church attendance, doctor/dentist visits, and social/recreational trips.

In many cases services have been organized, such as outreach programs which bring food or activities *to* the stay-at-home elderly, or organized activities to which the elderly can *go* or be brought. It is in this latter case that some forms of specialized transportation have been developed, including the celebrated "minibus," to be discussed later.

By the time of the first national Conference/Workshop on Transportation and Aging, organized in May 1970, at the primary instigation of Miss June Shmelzer, then Specialist on Aging of the United States Department of Health, Education, and Welfare, a number of such experiments had taken place. But more importantly, this first conference brought together specialists who had worked separately on different aspects of the problem: gerontologists, sociologists, urban planners, transportation specialists, and lay persons interested in aiding the elderly/handicapped. This conference pointed the way to a new view of this special problem.

The Handicapped

This group is the most difficult to estimate. The only arbitrary descriptors available are not in classifying numbers by salary or age, but in *extent* of handicap, or in *what constitutes* a handicap. A current estimate of numbers is shown in Table 1-3. This total of 6 million does not, of course, include those temporarily *disabled*. A more recent study places the total at 13,370,000 (Table 1-4). A figure including both permanently and temporarily disabled has been quoted as high as 40,000,000![22]

A recent study[23] defines a "transit-relevant, physically handicapped person" as

Any individual who, by reason of illness, injury, age, congenital malfunction, or other permanent or temporary incapacity or disability, is unable without special facilities or special planning or design to utilize mass transportation facilities and services as effectively as persons who are not so affected.[24]

Of the permanently handicapped, about one-third are employed. Most are potential users of public transportation. All of them should have, and want, the same opportunities the general public has, for working, shopping, social interchange, and recreation. But they need access to transportation which is free of the physical and economic (and psychological) barriers which keep them from traveling.[25] A study showed some of the reasons why this is true (see Table 1-5): *inconvenience* or *inappropriateness* appear to be the major problems, even beyond personal physical limitations and physical obstacles on the vehicles themselves.

Table 1-4 shows a total of 7,030,000 elderly handicapped (as opposed to 4

Table 1-3
Physically Handicapped, 1970

	Under 65 Years Old	Over 65 Years Old
Location		
Central city	600,000	1,300,000
Suburban	700,000	1,200,000
Rural	700,000	1,500,000
	2,000,000	4,000,000

Source: Manpower Report to the President, U.S. Department of Labor, transmitted to Congress, April 1971.

Table 1-4
The National Numbers of Handicapped with Transportation Dysfunctions[a]

Handicap Class	Elderly Handicapped	Nonelderly Handicapped	Total Handicapped
Noninstitutional			
Chronic conditions			
Visually impaired	1,460,000	510,000	1,970,000
Deaf	140,000	190,000	330,000
Uses wheelchair	230,000	200,000	430,000
Uses walker	350,000	60,000	410,000
Uses other special aids	2,290,000	3,180,000	5,470,000
Other mobility limitations	1,540,000	1,770,000	3,310,000
Acute conditions	90,000	400,000	490,000
Institutionalized	930,000	30,000	960,000
Totals	7,030,000	6,340,000	13,370,000

[a]1970 estimate of those people who can't use transit or who use transit with difficulty.

Source: *The Handicapped and Elderly Market for Urban Mass Transit*, Transportation Systems Center, NTIS PB 224 821, Department of Transportation, Cambridge, Mass., October 1973.

million, Table 1-3), and 6,340,000 "nonelderly handicapped" (as opposed to 2 million, Table 1-3). The differences lie in definition.

Of the 13,370,000, an estimated 5.3 million are unable to use transit at all. Table 1-6 breaks down this group. Those who "Can Go Out" constitute an additional transit market if transit were able to accommodate them.[26]

Table 1-7 gives those latest figures of both elderly and handicapped without double counting.

Few studies have been performed to *locate* the handicapped. At this writing, however, a survey is underway by the Tri-State Planning Commission in the metropolitan New York region to accomplish precisely that. There are indications that the elderly and the handicapped under 65 tend to be distributed in the U.S. in proportion to the general population. They range from 8 to 12 percent of the population in a number of both transit- and auto-oriented areas studied.[27]

A recent study measures the transportation problem for the *urban* handicapped (and the elderly), as seen in Figure 1-3, measuring transit availability within reasonable walking distance, and transit which cannot be used (in its present configuration).

Consideration for the handicapped, at least from an architectural standpoint,

Table 1-5
Percent of Handicapped Persons Who Do Not Use Bus by Degree of Handicap, Reason for Not Using Bus, and Employment Status

Degree of Mobility, Handicap, and Employment Status	Reason for Not Riding Bus		
	Personal Physical Limitations[a]	System Physical Obstacles[b]	Convenience or Appropriateness
Least handicapped:			
Employed	5	2	37
Unemployed	7	26	38
Moderately handicapped:			
Employed	25	10	25
Unemployed	23	33	26
Severely and very severely handicapped:			
Employed	37	50	12
Unemployed	36	29	13
Total:			
Employed	9	7	33
Unemployed	19	18	29

[a]Pain, slowness, and difficulty of movement, etc.

[b]Stairs, curbs, fast-closing doors, etc.

Source: Manpower Report to the President, U.S. Department of Labor, transmitted to Congress, April 1971.

goes back some years, perhaps most noticeably again to the post-World War II period, when increasing expertise of surgeons and then other medical specialists permitted those with various infirmities to survive and find an active life. The Federal Housing Authority was first in this country to systematize and regularize requirements for provisions permitting use of public buildings by the handicapped.

But it was the Bay Area Rapid Transit District (BARTD) in the San Francisco area, which began with a major project, the trend in considering the special needs of the handicapped in public transportation. And this major revision of already-final plans is due to the efforts essentially of one man, Mr. Harold Willson, of the Kaiser Foundation Medical Care Program, in Oakland, California. Mr. Willson was basically instrumental in having plans for the BARTD facilities revised to provide for their use by handicapped of all degrees, including wheelchairs (upon which Mr. Willson happens to be dependent himself).

Table 1-6
Handicapped Who Are Unable to Use Transit

	Under 65	65 and Over	Total
A. Can go out, but can't use transit	1,153,000[a]	1,153,000[b]	2,306,000
B. Can't leave home	878,000[a]	878,000[b]	1,756,000
C. Institutional	30,000[c]	930,000[c]	960,000
D. Acute conditions (temporary)	185,000[d]	50,000[d]	235,000
	2,246,000	3,011,000	5,257,000

A *minimum* of 5.3 million of the Nation's 13.4 million transit disadvantaged are probably unable to use transit.

[a]Social Security survey of the chronically handicapped, 1966.

[b]TSC estimate of equal incidence for over 65.

[c]Census of Population, 1970.

[d]HEW National Health Survey, 1970, estimated.

Source: *The Handicapped and Elderly Market for Urban Mass Transit*, Transportation Systems Center, NTIS PB 224 821, Department of Transportation, Cambridge, Mass., October 1973.

Table 1-7
Overview of Target Group Statistics

Total elderly		20,066,000
Total handicapped		13,370,000
There are significant overlaps		
Elderly and handicapped total (with no double counting)		26,406,000
This breaks down to three relevant mutually exclusive classes:		
Handicapped	Elderly	7,030,000
	Nonelderly	6,340,000
Elderly who are not handicapped		13,036,000
	Grand Total	26,406,000

Source: *The Handicapped and Elderly Market for Urban Mass Transit*, Transportation Systems Center, NTIS PB 224 821, Department of Transportation, Cambridge, Mass., October 1973.

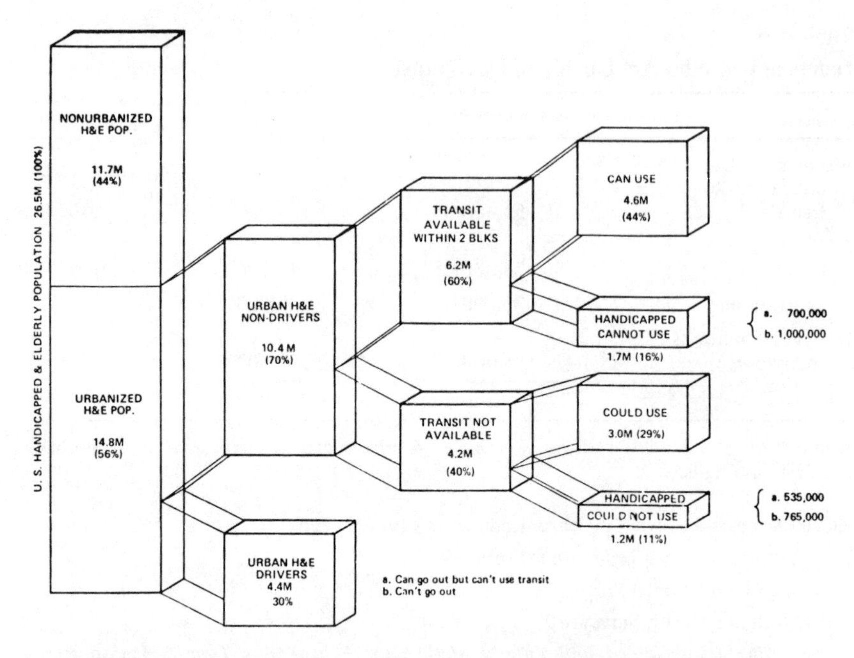

Figure 1-3. Sizing the Urban Transportation Problem for the Handicapped and Elderly. Source: *The Handicapped and Elderly Market for Urban Mass Transit*, Transportation Systems Center, U.S. Department of Transportation, Cambridge, Massachusetts NTIS PB 224 821. October 1973.

Since that time, however, and, indeed during and since the first Conference/Workshop on Transportation and Aging in 1970, the debate has been on the merits of improving or modifying existing transportation facilities to accommodate the handicapped, versus the institution of new, exclusive systems adapted to their needs.

2 Some Basic Concepts

This chapter considers transportation systems in the context of national, regional, and local[a] perspectives. Some of the criteria used to develop and evaluate transportation systems are discussed, briefly, to illustrate the issues relevant to the transportation-related problems of the disadvantaged. In this connection, emphasis is placed on the need to appraise the utility of the transportation system in relation to its effect on the low-income worker, the young, the aged, and the handicapped.

The Functional Scope of Transportation Networks

Transportation networks may be viewed as systems performing functions which affect national, regional, or local affairs. These functions can be separated into four sets of objectives. For example, a transportation system can be used to achieve:

1. Economic growth.
2. Land use service and land use development.
3. Modal balance.
4. Equitable opportunity for mobility to all persons.

Figure 2-1 illustrates the role of the transportation system in achieving the four objectives stated above, at the national, regional, or local levels. The solid lines show the primary roles of transportation in the achievement of a particular objective, while the broken lines describe the secondary roles of transportation. The number next to the flow lines tells how the transportation variable is entered into the analytical methods used to measure the impact of transportation in achieving the four objectives as they relate to the geographic level of analysis, that is, whether national, or local.

[a]*national* implies Nation or State;
regional implies metropolitan areas; and
local implies subareas within the metropolitan area.

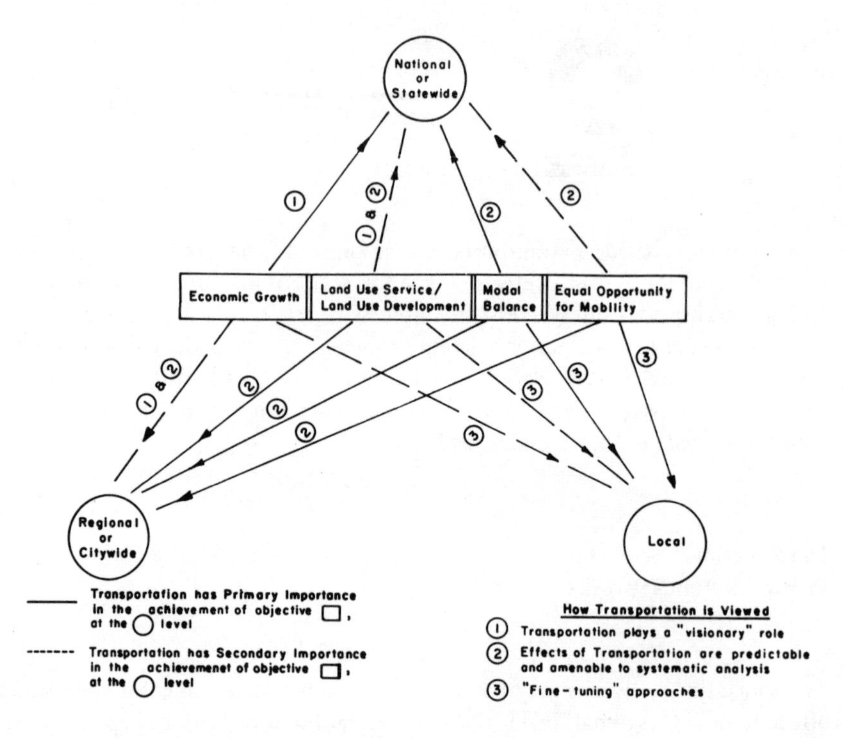

Figure 2-1. The Basic Functions of Transportation Systems

The Role of Transportation

Depending on the scope of an undertaking, the transportation system may be used at different levels of implementation to accomplish any of the above objectives. For example, to achieve economic growth at the national level, the transportation system is usually viewed as "visionary," or precedent-setting. Examples of this type are the Erie Canal in New York State, the Pennsylvania Turnpike, or the *Autostrada del Sole* in southern Italy. If the objective, however, is to improve the economic conditions of specific population groups at the local level, the use of a transportation system is restricted to "fine-tuning" approaches such as those employed in the Watts (California), Long Island (N.Y.), or Valley Transit District (Connecticut), transportation demonstration projects.

The Importance of Transportation

Figure 2-1 also shows that, at the regional level, transportation systems play a secondary role in the achievement of economic growth. But at the national level, transportation assumes a primary importance in the achievement of this objective.

The importance of transportation to the national economic growth of the United States, for example, is reflected by the huge investment in the National System of Interstate and Defense Highways, which was started in the mid-1950s, and in equally impressive airport projects. Also, most developing nations are still investing, even today, up to one-third of their gross national products in transportation.[1] The justification of large national investments in transportation resources is based on past experience, which has shown that improvements in accessibility of new areas accelerates economic growth by opening up new markets.

For most urban areas of the United States, however, the problem of inaccessibility is no longer the principal concern for economic growth. In fact, when compared to the accomplishments of the past 50 years, today's transportation improvements offer only marginal gains in average accessibility for most urbanized areas. For this reason, therefore, it appears that economic development and benefit/cost analysis alone can no longer be the primary justification for significant capital investments in urban transportation. This fact is supported by the evidence that political and private interests in many urban areas are primarily concerned with increasing the capacity of existing transportation networks to keep up with the demands of a growing population.

Regional Significance and Local Relevance of Past Transportation Planning Practice

The planning philosophy of the 1960s which has guided the regional transportation plans of today seems to be no longer applicable to the needs of the 1970s.

In the 1960s, regional transportation systems were centered on the goal of providing the highest possible level of mobility in urbanized areas. This philosophy, however, set a rather limited range of objectives against which transportation improvements were evaluated. Invariably, the transportation systems recommended by these studies evolved from criteria such as volume, capacity, speed, and desirable levels of service. The benefit-cost analyses used in evaluating alternative plans were, of necessity, confined to measuring the benefits and costs accrued to these mobility-oriented criteria.[2]

Webster's dictionary defines *mobility* as "ease of movement." To most transportation planners this has been translated to mean high travel speed and congestion-free highway travel. In recent years, however, the meaning of mobility has gained additional dimensions. Urban observers began to question the merit of the freeway-oriented solution in the achievement of increased mobility. They started questioning the effect of freeway construction on the physical structure and social needs of urban areas, and began pointing to serious shortcomings in the standard transportation system evaluation criteria widely used by federal, state, and ad hoc transportation agencies.

It is a fact that highways have increased the mobility of that large segment of the population which drives a car or has access to one.[3] Furthermore, highway solutions seem to have kept pace with increasing travel demand much better than one would imagine: "The hue and cry about cities choking and strangling to death is, for all practical purposes, simply an arm-waving exercise."[4] It can be shown, in fact, that traffic congestion has declined from decade to decade.

The additional mobility realized by auto-oriented travelers, however, has resulted, in many cases, in a decline in mobility for those persons who do not drive cars, or have no access to one. This is a large minority of the population, comprising the poor, the handicapped, the young, and the aged.

The increased suburbanization of people, jobs, and other activities was induced primarily by the extensive highway network built to serve the needs of the automobile. This universal highway momentum, which has apparently been responsible for the corresponding lack of public transportation service improvements, can be attributed to the practice of defining goals and objectives for single-mode transportation systems and facilities, rather than defining goals and standards in terms of the *user* of the total transportation system.[5]

The weakness of the limited scope of the transportation system evaluation process led to plans that, when time came for public discussion, were attacked by various groups as disruptive and lacking in regard for their immediate and long-range environmental and social effects. Thus, for example, the crosstown expressway in Philadelphia, the Lower Manhattan expressway, the entire Boston regional transportation plan, and more recently, interstate connections in Baltimore, freeways in San Francisco and New Orleans, have been kept from implementation by a public which felt the plans were not in harmony with local needs and values.[6]

The Need for New Transportation Planning Criteria

Transportation networks can no longer be viewed, therefore, as mutually exclusive systems, performing independent tasks in the achievement of a primary objective of national, regional, or local scope. Spillover effects are usually pervasive, and they can be simultaneously good and bad, depending on who is affected. The design and construction of the national system of interstate and defense highways, which is almost completed, has had a tremendous influence on the physical character, economic and social aspects of most urban areas of this nation. Although it has unquestionably been successful in the achievement of national and regional economic objectives, similar statements cannot be made when social and physical planning objectives of local scope are considered.

The past practice of neglecting the local needs of the region's subareas has led to weak plans. Transportation facilities in urban areas, therefore, should be viewed also as a means to alleviate the many problems which create great concern to the public and to its elected officials. For example, the problems of crime, unemployment, substandard housing and discrimination, while they are not directly related to transportation, can indeed be reduced or increased somewhat by the manner in which transportation developments are directed.

This emerging need, for relating the goals associated with the solution of urban problems to the requirements of urban transportation systems, is becoming the dominant issue for most transportation, land use, and city planners.[7] The federal government is beginning to respond to this need.[8]

Much research, no doubt, is still needed to convert the goals related to such social problems into transportation system requirements. And when one talks of transportation as an improving factor, invariably the question arises: Who does it benefit, and is the amount of benefit received worth the cost to someone else? But it is only through a systematic—albeit a painstaking—process that real plans are formulated.

The significance of the preceding discussion, as it relates to the topic of this book, is embodied in the question: How can transportation be used, and what types of transportation services are required, to improve the quality of life for the disadvantaged?

Community Cohesion and Transportation

"Community cohesion" is a term of relatively recent vintage which is intended to connote the invisible bonds within a social grouping which create a feeling of "community" beyond individual humanness and beyond family ties. Terms such as "sense of community," "neighborliness," and others have also been used. When discussed, such terminology is generally understood, but difficulty enters in attempting to define it in terms which will then lead to means of measurement.

Since it is an abstract term for a "feeling," the measures of community cohesion which have been tested are necessarily simplifications, but generally they tend toward such aspects of urban life which are of the greatest importance to precisely those population groups to which we address ourselves: the disadvantaged.

Measures of community cohesion include, among others:

1. Extent of pedestrianism.
2. Location and accessibility of community facilities.
3. Amount of "neighboring" and mutual help.
4. Knowledge of other individual families/individuals within a given area.
5. Recognition of geography of the area.

Pedestrianism

The indicator of community cohesion which includes the amount and type or purpose of walking in a community is of particular importance to the disadvantaged. The *young* who cannot use public transportation by themselves, or who cannot yet use private autos, must use the pedestrian mode or be "taken," or led, by adults. Thus they remain wedded to walking, or cycling, and the physical arrangement of a community either encourages or discourages walking. The greatest barrier to the free, unassisted movement of such children is traffic. The amount and velocity and other characteristics of traffic can be directly related to the ease or danger with which children (and others) cross streets, and therefore to the relative area of the community they cover and are familiar with.

Older youth are not inhibited from pedestrianism by traffic, generally, but their lack of "wheels" will relate to how far they are willing to walk or cycle to youth-oriented functions and facilities, and can thereby be related to such phenomena as delinquency, employment, and attitude.

The elderly are particularly dependent upon the pedestrian mode for economic reasons generally. But generally also, the elderly are cast, in this country, in two basic molds: either they are of the "old country," in attitude if not in fact, in eastern urban centers; or they are of the "little-old-lady-in-tennis-sneakers," Southern-California, liberated, motor-age. In the one case, close extended-family ties within short distances, colonies of aged in left-behind inner-city clusters, or a conscious coming together in areas with stores, doctors, and hospitals within easy distance, make walking especially important. In the other case, a good deal of driving may still be done, but walking is an important form of exercise and group activity.

In either case, walking is inhibited by the same problems of traffic confronted by the very young, compounded by problems of increasing physical limitation. In the case of traffic, special crossings for slow-moving citizens, plus refuge islands and areas, must be considered. In the case of physical impairment, walking is impeded by curbs, steps, street furniture, and crowds.

The handicapped of all ages, of course, find the latter array a problem, and curb cuts, ramps, and design and planning criteria can overcome them. Walking, or even self-propulsion in wheel chairs, remains, however, an important mode for the handicapped, both for exercise and for daily needs. If a person is mobile, his greatest mobility will be in walking or driving: the difficulties of using public transportation are well-documented. When he does not drive it is incumbent upon him to find his requirements and services within self-mobility distance. The poor are reduced to walking through necessity.

The obvious conclusion is: there is greater "community cohesion" where there are more elderly, children, handicapped, and poor.

Community Facilities

Ease of access to community facilities of all kinds, whether for shopping, government services, medical needs, or recreation, are of greatest importance to the disadvantaged.

"Neighboring"

A measure of neighboring is the willingness of people to help each other. Obviously the elderly, young, the poor and the handicapped are in greatest need of neighboring. Consequently they exhibit the greatest willingness to reciprocate in this manifestation of community spirit.

Knowledge of Neighborhood

In the knowledge of both the people and the geography surrounding them, the disadvantaged generally can be said to display the greatest scope, perhaps again through dire necessity and the limitations within which they operate.

It is true that individuals and small pockets of disadvantaged groups may be isolated, but generally even where this is the case it is most probable that such groups have knowledge of an area that has changed, or which is now unsafe for them, or which is inaccessible to them through immobility.

Community Cohesion and the Disadvantaged

It is apparent that the precise conditions which illustrate the ideal of a cohesive community are those which are basic necessities for the underprivileged. The great mass of "average" people can *afford* conditions of poor or low cohesion. They can *afford* to drive miles for a loaf of bread or a movie; they can *afford* the physical expenditure needed to take a bus or a train; they can *afford* the money it takes to do those and other things.

3 A Review of the Issues

Social and Economic Issues

The poor are poor for lack of money. Money in our society, at least money enough to take us out of poverty, is earned by working. The relationship of poverty to employment and transportation is the first issue.

The young are for a period of time left to their own devices yet expected, if not to contribute to society, to at least not disrupt it. This is the second issue.

The elderly don't get around as much as they used to. By choice or through necessity? This is the third issue.

The handicapped have a basic problem of wanting to be useful and complete citizens and getting to work. This is the fourth issue.

Employment, Unemployment, and the Poor

"In 1940, the suburbs contained 27 million people; 2 of every 10 Americans; 19 million fewer than the cities. Now they contain 76 million; almost 4 of every 10; 12 million more than the cities that spawned them."[1] This trend is expected to continue, unless new urban land development policies are instituted to effectively reverse the trend which is illustrated in Figure 3-1.

Because of such enormous population shifts, changes in patterns of nonresidential land uses (and thus jobs) also occurred. Industrial decentralization, which in effect started as soon as the railroad became established, accelerated at a very rapid pace due to the growing use of trucks, which made factories less dependent on sites near the railroads. Because of a growing dependence on the automobile for personal transportation (today four out of every five families own a car and 29 percent are multiple-car families),[2] availability of the labor supply did not present a problem. Other factors which contributed to the rapid decentralization of industry include:[3]

1. *Changing technology* which created decentralized industrial parks to replace the multistoried lofts provided for expansion.
2. Generous *parking space.*
3. The *government's policy* of permitting defense-connected industries to write off costs of new plants in a five-year period.

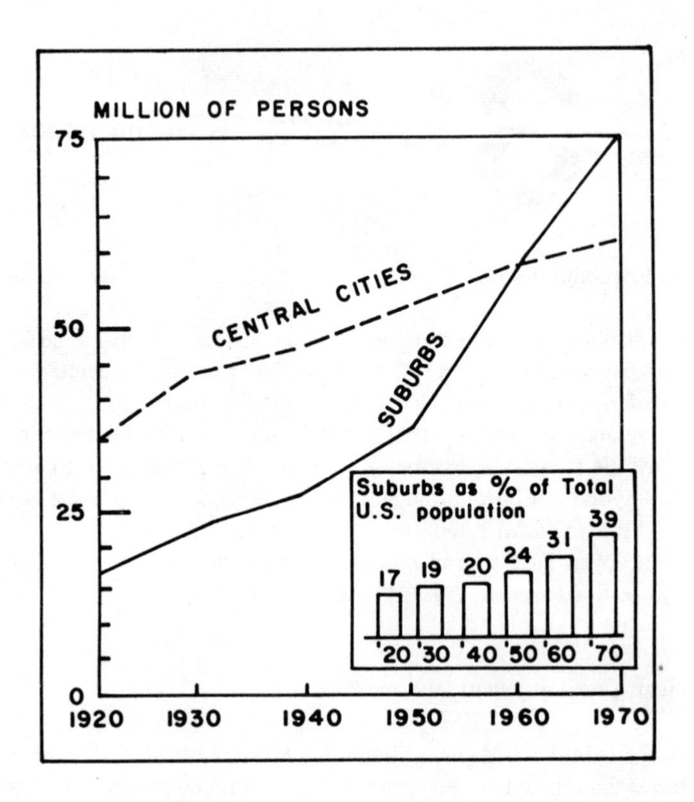

Figure 3-1. Suburban-Central City Population Trend, 1920-1970. Source: *The New York Times*, May 30, 1971. © 1971 by The New York Times Company. Reprinted by permission.

The impact of this decentralization pattern on employment opportunities was significant, as can be noted by the growth disparity which resulted between the central cities and suburban counties. Social Security data on employment in each county in the United States indicates that, for the Standard Metropolitan Statistical Areas[a] (SMSAs) with more than one county, total employment increased 13 percent from 1959 to 1965 in the central or main county, but it increased 22 percent in suburban counties. From 1960 to 1965, about half of the value of new construction in SMSAs for business purposes occurred outside the central cities. Percentages outside the central cities for major business categories were: Industrial, 62 percent; commercial stores, 52 percent; and office buildings, 27 percent.[4]

[a]The U.S. Bureau of the Census defines the SMSA as a county or a group of contiguous counties which contain (1) at least one city of 50,000 inhabitants or more, or (2) two cities with contiguous boundaries and with a combined population of at least 50,000. In cases where two or more adjacent counties each has a city of 50,000 inhabitants or more, *and* if the cities' limits lie within 20 miles of each other, they are included into a single SMSA if the two or more urban areas are economically and socially integrated.

Although the rapid growth of suburban business and industry has often been ascribed to a "flight of industry" from the cities, the limited information available indicates that the numbers of businesses actually moving to the suburbs have been relatively small. The rapid growth of employment there is largely due to new business establishments or expansion of existing plants.[5] In fact, employment growth in central cities has still kept up with the needs of the population living there.[6] Access to jobs, however, is not the same for all population subgroups.

These decentralization phenomena have resulted in a decline in average population densities of U.S. urbanized areas. As shown in Figure 3-2, between 1940 and 1960 the average density of urban areas decreased by 1,640 persons per square mile—from 5,870 to 4,230—and trends indicate a further decrease in density.[7]

The result of this continued dispersal of people and activities has been to make people more dependent on the automobile and, as data gathered in several areas[8] would indicate, average trip lengths have been increasing over time.

Thus the sheer size and rapid growth of population in metropolitan areas has helped to intensify commuting problems for all who live and work there. But for the urban poor, the ghetto dweller, the situation of job accessibility has deteriorated to the point where there is urgent reason for concern.

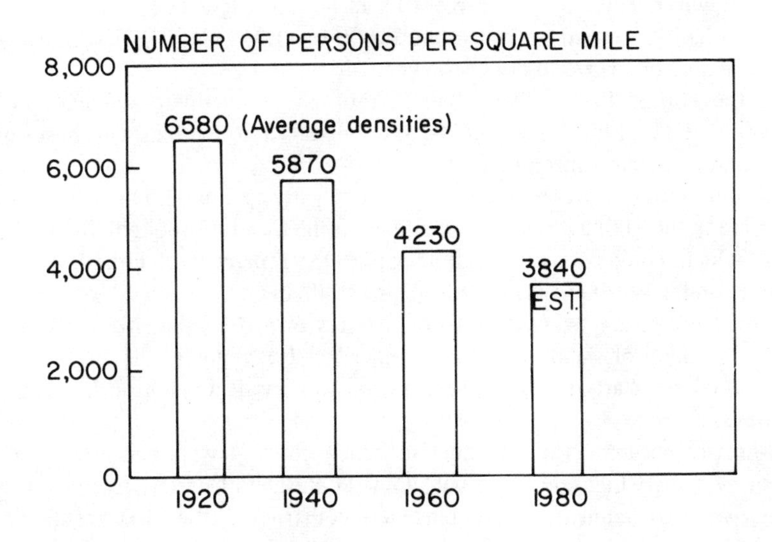

Figure 3-2. Decline in Average Population Densities of U.S. Urbanized Areas. Source: J.P. Pickard, "Dimensions of Metropolitanism," (Research Monograph 14, Urban Land Institute, 1967), pp. 48-53, reprinted with permission of ULI—the Urban Land Institute, 1200 18th Street, NW, Washington, D.C. 20036.

As was shown in Figure 3-1, between 1960 and 1970 population growth occurred almost exclusively in the suburbs. But the apparent stability of the central-city population is delusive. During the same period there was a sharp rise in the cities' black population (32 percent) and a decrease in the white population (5 percent); and, as Table 3-1 shows, the contrast was even more pronounced in metropolitan areas of one million or more population.

The nonwhite increase in population in the central cities was brought about, primarily, both by natural population growth and by a continuing influx of nonwhites, most of whom were from the rural South. These nonwhite migrants, who moved into the central cities, consisted primarily of unskilled, poorly educated individuals who came to the cities to find a job, improved educational opportunities, and a host of other amenities.

In many urban areas, however, the spacial arrangement of diverse activities is such that they are not equally accessible to all economic groups. The poor, who own few cars and depend primarily on public transportation for their daily travel, are the ones who feel the greatest constraint on their freedom of movement. Whereas the more affluent can with greater ease reach any activity in the urban area within a reasonable time, the poor face the constraints of cost and travel time which are associated with a desired journey. Consequently they are limited in their travel to areas which are well served by the public transportation system.

As shown in Table 3-2, 76 percent of all households with an annual income less than $1000, owned no car; in the $1000 to +1,999 class the percentage was 69; as income increases, so does car ownership.

In the United States, "less than half of all families with incomes under $4,000, half of all black households, and half of all households with heads over 65 years old, own no automobile."[9]

In some cities, however, the proportion of poverty households without a car far exceeds the U.S. average. For example, in the Central Brooklyn Model Cities Area (which contains over 404,000 persons), 91 percent of households with incomes under $4,000 have no car available to them.[10]

Furthermore, almost two thirds of the cars owned by the poor are over six years old, many of them "unusable jalopies."[11] For example, 20 percent of the cars owned by Watts residents were judged too unsafe for use on Los Angeles freeways.[12]

Primarily because of the manner in which cities grew, urban areas contain transit systems which are essentially Central Business District-oriented. At the time when most rapid transit systems were constructed, the CBD was the point where most people wanted to go, for work, for shopping, and even for recreational purposes. Today, however, most urban travel demand is *not* CBD-oriented. And, whereas in earlier times most of the poor worked in central-city industries, today these industries are becoming decentralized and therefore dispersed throughout the city or its metropolitan area. For example,

Table 3-1

Population in Metropolitan Areas, 1969, and Change, 1960 to 1969, by Place of Residence and Color (numbers in millions)

Place of Residence	1969				Change, 1960 to 1969			
		Number			Number		Percent	
	Total*	White	Negro	Percent Negro	White	Negro	White	Negro
All metropolitan areas	129.6	112.2	15.8	12.2	12.8	3.9	12.8	32.9
Central cities	58.7	45.4	12.5	21.3	−2.2	3.0	-4.8	32.0
Suburbs	70.9	66.8	3.3	4.7	15.0	.9	29.0	36.7
Metropolitan areas of 1,000,000 or more	70.3	59.6	9.8	13.9	5.7	3.0	10.5	44.0
Central cities	30.5	22.1	7.9	25.9	−2.0	2.3	−9.0	41.3
Suburbs	39.8	37.5	1.9	4.8	7.8	.7	26.5	56.5
Metropolitan areas under 1,000,000	59.3	52.6	6.0	10.2	7.1	.9	15.5	18.2
Central cities	28.2	23.3	4.6	16.4	−.1	.7	−.5	18.6
Suburbs	31.1	29.3	1.4	4.6	7.2	.2	32.4	17.0

*Minority races other than Negroes are included in the total, but not shown separately.

Note: Percents based on data in thousands.

Source: *Manpower Report of the President*, U.S. Department of Labor, transmitted to the Congress, April 1971, p. 85, Table 1.

Table 3-2
Automobile Ownership Within Income Groups, 1970

	Percentage Distribution of Spending Units[a]		
	Owns No Automobile	Owns 1 Automobile	Owns 2 or More
All spending units	18%	54%	28%
Money income before taxes[b]			
Under $1,000	75	22	3
$1,000-$1,999	59	40	1
$2,000-$2,999	50	43	7
$3,000-$3,999	40	54	6
$4,000-$4,999	30	61	9
$5,000-$5,999	25	66	9
$6,000-$7,499	14	71	15
$7,500-$9,999	8	66	26
$10,000-$14,999	4	55	41
$15,000 and over	4	36	60

[a]A spending unit consists of all persons living in the same dwelling and related by blood, marriage, or adoption, who pool their income for major items of expenses. Some facilities contain two or more spending units.

[b]Money income for previous year.

Source: *Survey of Consumer Finances*, conducted by the Survey Research Center of the University of Michigan.

67 percent of Central Brooklyn Model Cities Area residents work at locations outside the Manhattan CBD. And of those with no occupational skills, a greater proportion, 72 percent, worked outside the center city.[13]

Those who are poor depend almost entirely on public transportation to get anywhere beyond their walking radius. And, because public transportation, as it now exists, is not geared to handling decentralized travel, those persons who do not have access to an automobile find that employment, as well as other opportunities available to automobile owners, are not accessible to them.

This situation has been a factor in creating and sustaining the isolation of the poor, and has contributed to the social problem which now has begun to be the concern of government, as can be seen in the multitude of programs funded for the purpose of reducing the impact of poverty and to create new opportunities for improvement.

The rural poor have an enormous problem with transportation also. Costs are multiplied as distances increase and numbers of fares can be counted on one hand. Reliance on the automobile is even greater than in cities, and costs, of autos, of gasoline, of repairs and replacements, drive this ultimate means of transportation out of reach.

The Young: Being In-Between

The same statistics which show a huge increase in suburban populations and a relative stability or even decline in inner-city populations, relate to the transportation problems of the young. It is the same two major population groups, the middle-class suburbanites and the inner-city poor, which spawn the transportation difficulties of the young.

In the *suburbs* the young await the receipt of an automobile-driving license as a coming-of-age fetish; a ticket to freedom. But until that time they are at the mercy of poor community planning and parents' desires or propensities for ferrying them about in autos, or underwriting their use of usually inadequate public transportation.

Generally suburbs, since World War II, have been laid out as bedroom communities. No services or facilities were designed into the "developments" until recently. In such areas neighborhood facilities have been scaled to the automobile, and the "energy crisis" of 1974 has shown how delicate a construction it has been. In such an atmosphere, shopping has been centralized with the phenomenon of the "suburban shopping center," an island surrounded by acres of parked cars, becoming the center of attractions.

Schools are more auto-centered also, including the elementary school. The elementary school, which has been the touchstone of the definition of a neighborhood to the urban planner, is no longer a neighborhood-centered facility. First through consolidation justified on the basis of centralization and spread-suburb low densities (acceptable as long as many children could be bussed), then because of additional bussing required by racial integration politics, the elementary school is now designed to cover more than the easy-walking-distance of city planning standards of twenty years ago.

The high school then has an even greater "catchment" area; and especially in western states we have the phenomenon of high-school students driving, individually, to school. Public transit is poor and little-used, both as a cause and as a result of the auto-centered society.

The suburban shopping center has become a focal point for teen- and pre-teenagers in the suburbs. Whether they drive themselves there or hitchhike, it is a focal point otherwise lacking in the generally bleak suburbs, lacking in the kind of density which results in "hangouts" in more urbanized areas.

In the *inner-city* it is true that, if facilities are not within short distances (in many cases they are), then much better public transit facilities exist. But then also the young have less hope of "graduating" to car-ownership, and the cost of public transit is of greater moment and importance. Fewer cars owned by adults means less reliance on hitchhiking; and crime and fear of crime have their effect on this mode of travel also.

Finally, while mass transit is more available and offers more coverage, school-reduced fares apply only to school travel, and the general lack of money, coupled with inflation and rising fares, dampens the potential movement of youth. Again, a lack of places to go and a means to get there, add to the spiral in social and psychological costs.

Rural youngsters find their mobility problems magnified. School busing must cover greater distances, and the auto is relied upon for entertainment or work. This problem is eased somewhat by the fact that driving ages are generally lower in rural areas, but for the rural poor this is little consolation.

The Elderly and Mobility

Studies show a decline in "life space" with increasing age.[14] An illustration of this concept is seen as Figure 3-3. The question is, is this retraction of life space a desired one on the part of the elderly? Or is it a result of reduced physical and pecuniary circumstance? As will be seen in the discussion of demonstration projects for the aged, below, these questions still can arise, even while many programs are successful. The small life space of the child (see Figure 3-3) can be seen as a result of immaturity in capability, interest, and finances. The greater life space of adulthood can be seen as a result of both *necessity* (work) and *desire* (recreation, tourism, money to spend). The reduced life space of the aged may be seen as either necessity (reduced physical powers and financial means), or *desire* (fears of falling, of muggings, of "not keeping up," *anomie*, etc.). Apparently it is a combination of both, or, at least, for some a necessity, for some a desire.

It is in the urban and suburban areas of our country that the transportation problems of the elderly have come to the fore. In the suburbs they share, to a greater and greater extent as age and infirmities increase, the incapacity of young children to drive themselves about. They also share, if they have developed physically disabling handicaps, the difficulties which very young children have in boarding buses, negotiating "normal" stair riser heights, and other such barriers. And finally, they join the young in their reduced financial circumstances, generally, limiting further the capacity for mobility.

Where there is a marked difference between the young and the old, however, is in physical capacity, and in time. Physical capacity (and the mental confidence which goes with it) allows the young to find alternatives like hitchhiking and walking, although walking is not alien to the elderly, as will be pointed out. Time, on the other hand, has produced a different attitude among the aged as concerns mobility, outside interest, desire for transportation, and familiarity with places to go and things to do. Of the previous generation, many of the elderly were immigrants with circumscribed life spaces; the mobility explosion of the 1950s and 1960s will make the next generation of elderly as different in outlook and habit as the generation of today's youth.

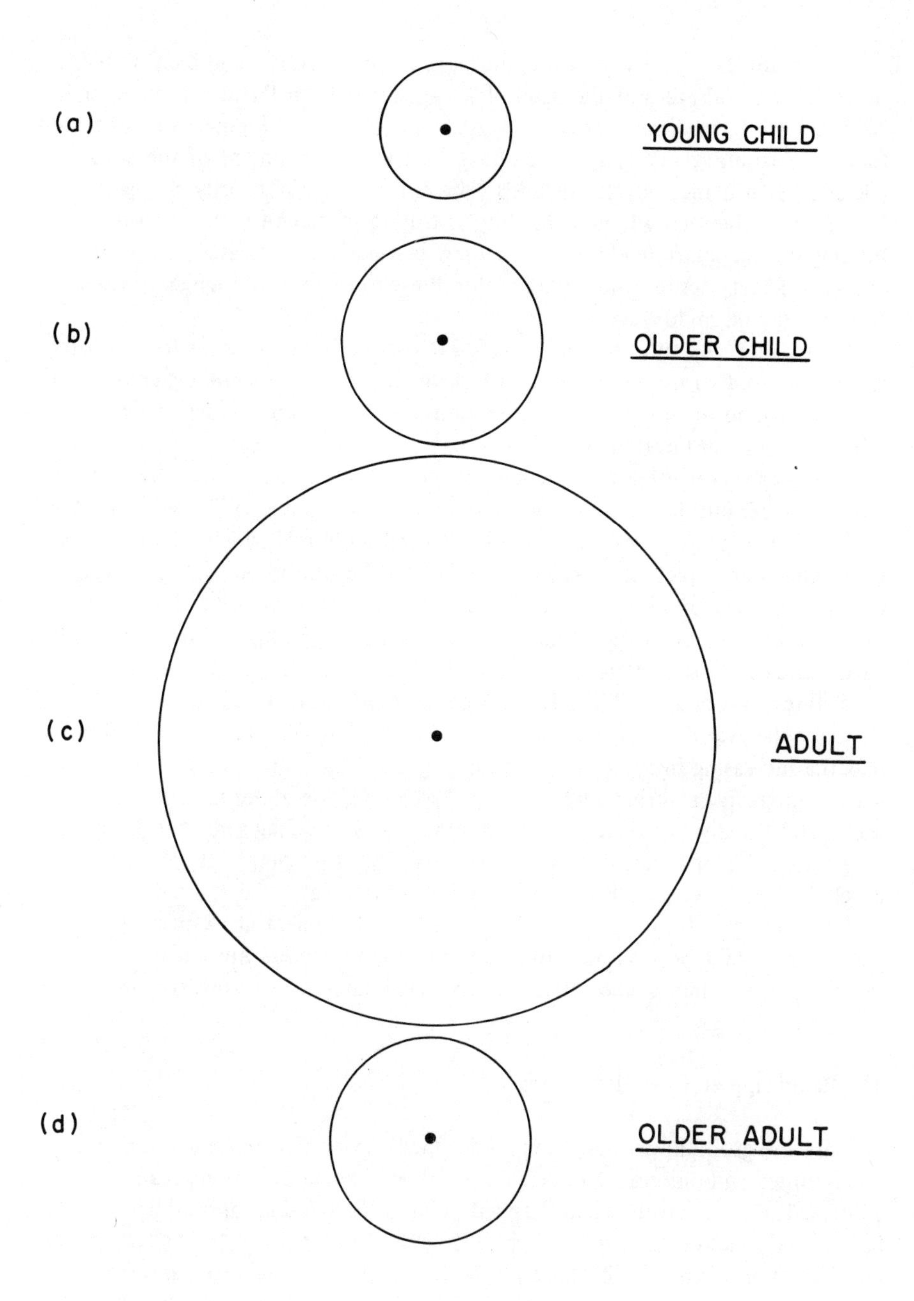

Figure 3-3. Life Space of Ages of Man

This is not to say that there are not many little old ladies (and men) in tennis shoes driving 200 miles at the drop of a hat, not only in Pasadena, but even in New Milford, Connecticut, or Dothan, Alabama. But the differences of three and four generations, generations which have seen the development of the automobile and the airplane, and the decline of the railroads, are not easily shrugged off. It remains to be seen whether mobility is truly a matter of early exposure and training on a generational level, or whether, as some have indicated, it is simply a loss of interest, desire, and occasion for the extent of travel which existed in one's youth and middle age.

At any rate, the suburbs offer a lack of neighborhood facilities to an elderly generation used to urban cohesion; a lack of mass transit on the order of what had been found in the cities; and even on those facilities that exist, the physical difficulties inherent in their use.

The elderly remaining in the cities are generally those left essentially on their own, left behind by children who improved themselves by moving to the suburbs. They may have remained in old neighborhoods which in earlier days were tenement copies of European towns, with neighborhood facilities within walking distance, or a job at the end of a trolley-car or subway (or elevated) line. Today, they remain in the neighborhood, but the languages on the storefronts have changed; supermarkets, at greater distances, have replaced neighborhood food stores, and other facilities for visiting or entertainment are a chore to reach. Here it is the ever-rising cost of transportation which makes travel more difficult, plus the increasing infirmities of age making it a longer walk to a transit station; fear of mugging in alien neighborhoods restricting the time of day of such a walk; and finally, difficulties in climbing stairs, holding onself against the acceleration of insensitive bus drivers, and the full range of physical and psychological drawbacks to be confronted in mass travel.

The rural elderly are perhaps the most housebound of all, especially when poor or part of a poor family. Bus trips to activity centers must necessarily be more expensive than in the suburb or city, while incomes are consistently lower.

The Handicapped: Getting to Work

Because the group known as "the handicapped" spans all economic levels and all age, ethnic, and interest groups, all social and economic issues can also be addressed. By age groups, handicapped children (depending upon degree) must have special handling to special schools; older children and adults need special consideration in the use of either public transport or specialized transportation; the handicapped elderly are the "elderly" to whom we address ourselves here.

Handicapped adults have special problems with transportation. Many of them have jobs, and salaries run the range of salaries of general economic levels. But if the handicapped person has decided, or has had decided for him, that he cannot use public transportation or a personal car, his cost, for specialized transport, can be astronomical. For instance, it is not uncommon for handicapped individuals to pay forty to sixty dollars *per week* for transportation, usually in a limousine or other taxi-type car service arrangement.

But the need of the handicapped individual for transportation is *at least* equal to his "normal" equivalent in the population. If he is neither young nor old, he still has desires and needs to go shopping, to go to entertainment and recreation areas, to educational institutions, to medical and dental expertise. If his transportation bill for *getting to work* is in the \$50/week area, he can spare little more for other necessary and desirable transportation. Especially important to the handicapped is movement to and from training and rehabilitation centers.

The Decline of Transit Service

Effects on the Poor

In many urban areas the almost universal dependency on the automobile for personal transportation has shut the poor out of opportunities and has been a major factor in the rapid decline of public transit patronage practically everywhere in the country (see Figure 3-4).

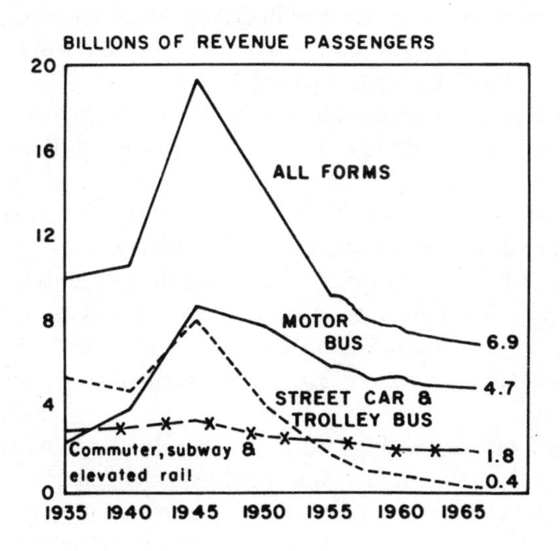

Figure 3-4. Trends in Revenue Passengers of Urban Public Transportation. Source: *Transit Fact Book*, 1967, American Transit Association; *Statistics of Railroads of Class I in the United States*, August 1967, Association of American Railroads.

In view of the changing conditions of urban form, urban mass transit systems have not responded to meet the needs of changing conditions:

1. Routes have tended to remain constant despite large population shifts and significant changes in land use.
2. Central city mass transit service does not continue beyond city boundaries.
3. Transit charters and legal restraints further limit expansion of the transit systems which could serve suburban growth.

The large numbers of poverty-stricken families that reside in the cities are faced with a public transit system which is progressively deteriorating, both physically and functionally.

The transportation system serving the people of an urban, suburban or even rural area is a vital force in assisting in the achievement of social and economic goals designed to improve the quality of life. This should be true not only for the middle and upper classes, business, industry, and commerce, but also for the low-income members of our society.

Since public transportation typically (today) does not lead, but *follows* urban settlement, it can be argued that the poor, on the whole, constitute the group receiving minimal gains from the large volume of highway construction which has taken place in urban areas during the last two decades.

In fact, the benefits provided to the vast majority by the rapid expansion of the highway system may have resulted in *dis*benefits to the working urban poor. New manufacturing and wholesale jobs have shifted from the traditional center-city sites to the less congested areas of the metropolis, where access by existing public transportation is either costly or excessively time-consuming.

For example: the straight-line distance between South Central Los Angeles and Santa Monica, an employment center, is 16 miles. By automobile the travel time is approximately 1/2 hour, but by public transit it takes one hour and 50 minutes, requires three transfers, and costs 83 cents one way.[15]

Similarly, if one travels by mass transit from the Bedford-Stuyvesant area of central Brooklyn, New York City, it is easier to reach points in the Bronx, some 16 miles away (travel time 45 minutes), than it is to go to nearby industrial employment centers located in Queens, four miles away, and requiring 60 minutes.[16]

A study[17] of the travel habits of Model Cities Residents in Central Brooklyn, New York, provides some insights into the travel characteristics of the poor for the basic daily functions of *working, shopping, health*, and *recreation.* The study concluded that the travel desires of the poor are *not* different from those of the more well-to-do public. Indeed, the poor exhibit the same preferences for shopping, recreation, health, and work. How they achieve these objectives, however, is quite different from the pattern observed for the nonpoor. The poor are constrained in their mobility both by their economic predicament and the physical characteristics of the transit system.

1. *They travel less*, simply because they have less money to spend.
2. They are further *constrained in mobility* when they reside in areas requiring multiple fares to ride the transit system.
3. They *rely almost exclusively on public transportation* for mobility, and are therefore dependent upon a unimodal system of transportation.
4. Although they have exhibited *work travel patterns similar to those of the nonpoor,* this is a reflection more of the land-use service characteristics of the transit system than on the choice of work destinations.
5. *Trips* made for shopping, medical reasons, or recreation *involve, on the average, a longer travel time* for the poor than the nonpoor.
6. The poor *travel to less distant places* than the nonpoor when the trips are made for shopping or medical reasons.
7. The poor *have a reduced choice of opportunities* for shopping, health care, recreation, or jobs.

Based on these findings, it appeared that several areas of improvement were possible to remove some of the barriers which inhibit the mobility of low-income persons who live in poverty such as the CBMC area. Some recommendations which would produce immediate results are:

1. Elimination of the multiple-fare system.
2. Increase of off-peak operations for some important routes.
3. Allowing group riding in taxis to reduce costs.
4. Installation of new transit routes from major transit terminals to points of industrial job concentrations, major shopping areas, hospitals and clinics, and regional recreational areas.
5. Improving the coordination of arrivals and departures of transit vehicles at major interchange points, especially during off-peak hours.

For the more distant future, however, more effective solutions should be implemented. Such solutions would not constitute the kind of patchwork remedies which were suggested above, but instead should concentrate on the necessary attributes which a public transit system should have to serve the increasing dispersal of activities in metropolitan areas.

The use of the conventional bus in a mass transit operation is limited in applicability to corridors of higher densities, which are usually radial in character. The standard bus, moreover, is not suitable to serve nonradial travel, especially when it operates on a fixed-route pattern. In these cases what is needed is a mass transit vehicle which most nearly approaches the attributes of the private automobile. Thus, the development of a low-cost "door-to-door" transit system, operated on the principle of Dial-A-Bus, might provide the appropriate solution to the mobility needs of low-income persons. Such a system should be coordinated with conventional mass transit vehicles at all major interchange points, and should penetrate the low-density areas where significant job opportunities and other activities are located.

For smaller cities the problems of the poor are even more severe. Kidder,[18] in her studies of Greensboro, North Carolina, found that carless, poor individuals are "denied social services because of transportation difficulties."

Effects on the Young

The decline of transit service, being a decline of both *quality* of service, and of *availability* of some services, has had its effects on the young as well. On the one hand we find a general decline in amenity which can be said to be affected by the young: we have the example of the rise in vandalism and the application of "graffiti" to new (and old) transport rolling stock. On the other hand it is true that a declining, degraded environment, such as that of many public transportation facilities throughout the U.S., must have its psychological effect on the user, and especially the young user. Noise, stench, ugliness, violence, as elements of daily "environment," cannot fail to affect the impressionable young. Many of these same young are exposed to these factors in their daily home environment, and are reducing the environment of the transit facility to the level with which they are generally familiar. So we are confronted with social effects and social symptoms.

Another aspect of the effects of the general decline in transit service on the younger population is simply in a lesser availability of service, especially during off-peak, or non-rush-hour, periods. For attending schools beyond walking distance, we have the use of transit facilities by children during morning peak hours and during afternoon nonpeak hours. During the morning rush hour they are adding to insupportable crowding, and during the afternoon they are affected by reductions in bus/train availability, a reduction in off-peak periods which can mean greater concentration of school children on public transit vehicles in the afternoons. In inner-city situations this can lead to antisocial behavior.

Effects on the Elderly

The decline in transit service as it affects the elderly again seems to strike at this group in two general areas: service and amenity, or environment. In *service* it is the area of greatest decline, the off-peak periods, which are most material and useful to the elderly. The elderly, who decline in physical capacity for quick movement, or whose changed psychological outlook removes them from the need or desire for competition with others, want to avoid the crowding and standardized movement of rush-hour traffic. Off-peak periods represent their means of making trips for all purposes: visiting, shopping, education, even medical. The decline in such services means longer waits in unpleasant, even hostile, locations. With buses it may mean waiting on street corners in bad weather, in desolate areas, in areas frequented by muggers (who often prey on the elderly), for long and tiring periods. With rapid transit it will mean waiting on desolate platforms, again as prey to muggers.

In another area the decline of transit service has meant a decline in new and novel improvements to public transit vehicles, whether bus or rail, which might have aided their use by the aged (and the handicapped). The buses and trains that have been replaced have not (except for BART) been constructed with a view to accommodating the elderly and handicapped.

Effects on the Handicapped

Effects of the general decline in transit service are perhaps more difficult to discern in considering the handicapped. With one group of the handicapped, those who have never considered themselves capable of using public transportation, there has been no ostensible impact. Yet, just as a lack of improvement to public systems is one symptom of that general decline, so can we see that making no effort to *include* this group in the ridership is as much an effect of that general decline.

With the other group of handicapped, those who have been utilizing mass transportation, the effect is equal to effects on the aged population. Reductions in service greatly limit the mobility of this grouping, and they are just as open to attack by the criminal element as are the debilitated aged. Of course, decline in maintenance and operating standards, and a lack of general upgrading or improvement, have had their effect on this segment of the population as well as others.

Thus, there is great need for providing transportation improvements for the disadvantaged, because the existing systems are not responsive to their basic requirements for travel. Failure to respond to these needs will deteriorate the social efforts aimed at reducing the gap between them and the rest of the population.

4 A Review of Some Demonstration Projects

The "Demonstration Project" is the mechanism chosen, generally by the federal funding agencies, to test an idea or concept in the field of transportation. In the past twenty years, a number of such projects have taken place. After the Watts riots (and Watts-type riots) of the 1960s there were a number of attempts at linking availability of transportation to employment. While there have been no special projects for the "youth" of the nation as a whole, there has been money for school bussing, for half-fare school fares, and the like. In recent years there has been an interest in providing transportation, or aid in mobility, to the elderly, or to the "elderly and handicapped." Sometimes this aid is informal, and a part of a larger program, as on "outings" or travel to senior centers. At other times there have been experiments in drawing out the transit-disadvantaged specifically to a transportation mode.

Projects for the Unemployed

The impact brought about by the studies conducted by the McCone Commission and the South Central Area Welfare Planning Council concerning the Watts riots of the summer of 1965, motivated the federal government to finance special transit services in those urban areas where the need for them was sorely visible. The "era" of bus demonstration projects in low-income areas started with the Transportation-Employment Project for South Central and East Los Angeles, popularly known also as the Watts area of Los Angeles.

Although the immediate purpose of this and other similar projects was to provide the needed linkage between low-income workers and jobs, the overall goal included evaluation of programs and development of recommendations which would add to the existing knowledge of mass transportation techniques so that the results could be applicable in solving the mass transportation problems in other areas.

Projects of this type were initially funded and administered by the Department of Housing and Urban Development (HUD) and are now currently administered by the Urban Mass Transit Administration (UMTA) of the U.S. Department of Transportation.

Los Angeles

The project area consists of ten major communities, located in an area of 46 square miles, and containing a population of 500,000 persons. Seven of these communities constitute South Central Los Angeles and three constitute East Los Angeles.

In general, the communities differ in their geographic proximity to the important activities and facilities in the Los Angeles metropolitan area. Similarly, differences also occur in the types of problems encountered, and in the social and economic make-up of the population.

The public transit service, which is supplied by a bus network, ranges from a relatively "dense" grid in the Avalon, Central and Boyle Heights areas, which are adjacent to downtown Los Angeles and the Central Manufacturing District, to the widely spaced bus route systems in Willowbrook and City Terrace.

Although the project area communities are generally closer to downtown Los Angeles than most other communities of the Los Angeles Metropolitan area, this proximity advantage has little meaning when one considers that most employment, recreation, and other facilities are widely dispersed in the Los Angeles area.[1] The proximity to the CBD in this case then provides access to only a fraction of the total range of activities and opportunities available to the residents.

Metropolitan Los Angeles is perhaps the most automobile-oriented large city in the United States. Urban growth there has apparently taken place on the assumption that a car is available to anyone and, as a result, accessibility to opportunities in the area becomes very difficult if anything other than a car is used. This problem is evidenced by the fact that 83 out of 100 families in Los Angeles have at least one car available.[2]

The communities in the project area, however, have much lower car ownership as indicated in Table 4-1.

Table 4-1
Car Ownership in Los Angeles Project Area Communities

Communities	Households Without Automobile (percent)
South Central Los Angeles	
Central	47.8
Avalon	47.4
Exposition	34.5
Green Meadows	27.3
Watts	42.1
Florence	33.2
Willowbrook	20.6
East Los Angeles	
Boyle Heights	40.6
City Terrace	26.3
Belvedere	30.8

The majority of the residents had income below the poverty level and the unemployment rate among the labor force of the community was about 12 to 15 percent, or approximately three times that of the Los Angeles Metropolitan area.

Four major deficiencies in public transportation in the area were identified by the project staff. These were:[3]

1. Lack of transfers between the lines of the Southern California Rapid Transit District (SCRTD) and the lines of the five other municipal and private operators serving the project area.
2. Lack of transfers between SCRTD local and interurban lines or between interurban lines outside of the Los Angeles inner zone.
3. Failure in providing an adequate public transportation system capable of serving a grid pattern development which is primarily automobile-oriented.
4. The transit information program does not provide adequate information for those who need the service most.

A number of projects were initiated to remedy these deficiencies. The major emphasis of these projects centered on providing low-cost transportation from the project areas to centers of employment that could not easily be reached by existing public transportation.

Long Island, New York

The problem of the carless who are not adequately served by public transportation is not limited to cities. In suburban areas there is frequently no public transit to serve communities where large numbers of the poor live. In areas where transit lines are available, they do not necessarily serve the large concentrations of industries where employment opportunities particularly suitable to the unskilled are plentiful. Instead such lines are operated along corridors of maximum activities and usually are directed towards the business districts.

The existing public transportation facilities in Nassau and Suffolk Counties do not serve the needs of the carless traveler well. The Long Island Railroad provides service to New York City, but is limited in its usefulness for intracounty trips. Existing bus services are infrequent, uncoordinated and expensive. Most of the poverty areas were served, if at all, by routes which did not make direct connections to any of the employment concentrations in the counties. In Nassau, most trips to employment concentrations involved one, two or more transfers, with accompanying multiple fares. In most cases, transfers involved excessive time loss. In Suffolk County, most employment concentrations were completely unserved by public transport.[4]

Concurrent with the actual operation of the bus demonstration project in many poverty areas of Long Island, the Tri-State Transportation Commission authorized a study[5] to provide a better understanding of the problems encountered in the job market by both industry and the low-income labor force.

A sample of seven poverty areas was selected for analysis. Four were located in Nassau County (Rockville Centre, Westbury, Roosevelt, Long Beach) and three in Suffolk County (Bay Shore, Brentwood, Central Islip).

A high rate of unemployment was found in the seven poverty study areas. On the average, unemployment was higher in Suffolk County (21 percent), and among welfare households the unemployment rate was about 58 percent. In general, the unemployment rate was higher for the female labor force, especially for welfare households. Households reporting income had the lowest unemployment rate (9.2 percent in Nassau and 19.5 percent in Suffolk). However, the median household income for these households was lower in Nassau than in Suffolk ($4,090 vs. $4,650), a finding which is apparently attributable to the higher rate of employed workers per family in Suffolk County (1.51 per household) than in Nassau County (1.26 per household). The employed labor force consisted primarily of unskilled and semiskilled persons. However, the proportion of skilled persons was also significant (see Table 4-2).

The proportion of poverty area households with no car available ranged from 15 percent in Brentwood to 67 percent in Long Beach. Public transportation, therefore, was an important means of travel for many workers and the role of unemployment in the seven poverty areas was found to be related to the availability of a car in the household and to the quality of public transportation available (see Table 4-3).

The above results show that, although unemployment is lowest in those areas of higher car ownership, the converse may not be true. In fact, in Rockville Centre, where car ownership is low but where bus service is of highest quality, unemployment rates are lower than in Long Beach which has a similar car ownership but one-half as much bus service as Rockville Centre.

The PIB Study[a] included the participation of Health and Welfare Council of Nassau County and the Economic Opportunity Council of Suffolk County, which were under contract to the Tri-State Commission. The role of the

Table 4-2
Distribution of Occupational Skills in Poverty Target Areas

	Skill Classification (percent)				
County	Sec.-Cler.	Skilled	Semiskilled	Unskilled	Not Reported
Nassau	6.5	17.2	36.8	28.5	11.0
Suffolk	3.3	14.0	60.7	19.7	2.3

[a]It should be noted that the employers' surveys were conducted in 1968. At that time economic conditions were "good" compared to the present (1974) situation.

Table 4-3
Unemployment Occurrence in Seven Poverty Areas

Poverty Areas	Households Without Automobiles (in percent)	Number of Buses, Morning Peak	Unemployment Rate
Nassau County			
Rockville Centre	61	40	24%
Westbury	44	6	31%
Roosevelt	42	18	24%
Long Beach	67	20	43%
Suffolk County			
Bay Shore	50	6	31%
Brentwood	15	8	18%
Central Islip	23	6	16%

Source: *Transportation Requirements and Characteristics of Low-Income Families as Related to Job Availability in Non-CBD Employment Concentrations.* Final Report to the Tri-State Transportation Commission, Polytechnic Institute of Brooklyn, December 30, 1968.

Councils in the study was to refer job applicants to those firms, contacted by PIB, which had job openings.

A total of 2,700 firms was contacted. These firms were selected so that they could easily be identified as centers of employment by the unemployed poverty area resident. Twenty-seven such centers of employment resulted. Some of these had an official identification, i.e., the Plainview and Engineer's Hill Industrial Parks and the Grumman Plants in Bethpage; other centers were groups of industrial-commercial complexes such as those located along Route 110 in Farmingdale and along Sunrise Highway in Lynbrook, Rockville Centre, and Freeport.

The largest number of job openings was found in the unskilled category. These accounted for more than twice the number of openings in the semiskilled or skilled categories; 10 times the number of clerical jobs available; and approximately 30 times the number of job openings in the secretarial category.

The findings of the industrial survey indicate the importance of transportation on *job openings.* It was found that firms located along the Long Island Railroad Corridor had lower-than-county average job openings in unskilled positions. Plants located along the LIRR Corridor have the most convenient transportation access to the labor force not necessarily because of the railroad service[b] but because many bus lines connect with trains at several stations.

[b]The poor used the LIRR very infrequently.

With respect to *labor turnover* most employers in the two counties have retained their labor force for over one year (see Table 4-4).

The extent to which turnover may be viewed as a function of transportation service to these plants is not clearly recognizable, however. Other factors such as wage levels, working conditions, employee benefits, opportunities for advancement, which differ from firm to firm were not well documented and did not permit an assessment of the transportation variable in its effect on labor turnover differentials.

Evaluation

The Los Angeles and Long Island demonstration projects were undertaken for the purpose of providing public transportation services to people who, because they are poor, do not have the means of owning their own automobile. The prime objective of the bus demonstration projects was to provide a needed means of mobility to low-income workers so that new job opportunities might be made available to them. The outcome of such effort was to be reflected in higher employment among the unskilled labor force.

Upon the termination of demonstration subsidies, however, the most important criterion considered for the justification of continuing the project routes was the financial success of the operation. Financial success was based on the economics of route operation and did not include the benefits derived by the various population segments who rode the buses.

Table 4-4
Labor Stability by County

	Percentage of Work Force			
	Nassau		Suffolk	
Length of Employment	Total Five Levels	Unskilled Only	Total Five Levels	Unskilled Only
More than 12 months	79	55	50	64
9-10 months	9	9	12	6
6-9 months	3	18	13	5
3-6 months	4	9	12	11
Less than 3 months	5	9	13	14
	100	100	100	100

Source: *Transportation Requirements and Characteristics of Low-Income Families as Related to Job Availability in non-CBD Employment Concentrations.* Final Report to the Tri-State Transportation Commission, Polytechnic Institute of Brooklyn, December 30, 1968.

Apparent inconsistencies resulted in the transition that occurred from the initial project objectives and the criteria used to justify the merit of continuing the projects.

Obviously these projects were not initiated by bus operators who were attracted to these areas by a potential profit. But they were, in fact, motivated by the need for a public service in the area. Social benefits played an important role in evaluating the merit for undertaking a demonstration project. Yet when subsidy funds were used up the only criterion that determined if a line should be continued was whether or not it rendered a profit to the operator.

It appears that the fallacy of this approach was due, to a great extent, to the inadequacy of project monitoring by the staffs of the demonstration programs. Reports published by the demonstration agencies, for example, do not contain detailed information which would be necessary to justify public subsidy. The two important aspects to be considered in this regard are:

1. Identification of the beneficiaries of the service.
2. The extent to which they are being helped.

One obvious result of the two studies was the conclusion that poverty area bus services cannot be expected to be financially successful. Even the routes of relatively high ridership such as the Century Blvd. line in Los Angeles, and Route B in Nassau County, are unable to cover costs.

It is clear then, that this cannot be used to evaluate the success or failure of the project, without also considering the service which is provided to poverty area residents. The example of the Century Blvd. line is a striking one. On the basis of reported statistics, the line carries 3,000 passengers per day, half of which originate in the poverty sector. Over 70 percent of these use the service for work trips. Assuming that each person accounts for two passengers (assuming that a person makes the round trip in one day), this suggests that over 500 poverty-area residents use the line each day to get to work. The ridership survey results of the Nassau-Suffolk study give an even more graphic indication of the service these routes provide for the low-income community. Of those questioned, 72 percent indicated that they had obtained their jobs as a result of the project routes, and 69 percent indicated that they could not keep their job without the routes.

These figures tend to give credibility to the fact that these routes serve a vital community function, one which must be evaluated for its own sake, exclusive of whether or not the line is financially successful. However, this data is not enough to completely evaluate the beneficial effects of the improved transport on the community. For example, it would be of great importance to place some economic value on the service to the community. For this, it is not alone sufficient to determine that 500 persons from a poverty area use the Century Blvd. line to commute to work. Data is required as to how many of the 500 riders actually obtained jobs as a result of the line, and for example, how many of these were formerly receiving welfare payments. Individuals who now use the line because it is less expensive and more convenient than their previous mode experience an economic benefit in terms of increased purchasing power due to reduced cost. Also, those who have obtained better jobs as a result of the route experience economic benefit which must be quantified. These are just a few of the quantifiable aspects which can, admittedly with some difficulty, be measured and evaluated. If the demonstration projects are to be of universal use, such data, which is now lacking, should be studied.

A second major consideration of a demonstration program concerns the operational characteristics of the trips being made in the bus (these are trip distribution, trip length, time of day, etc.) and the possibility of other alternatives to bus service. Such analyses were made in the PIB study for Long Island, but their utility was limited in application since funds were already committed to bus oriented improvements. However, in that study it was shown that bus transportation improvements did not provide the operational flexibility needed in low-density areas and it was concluded that a taxi or jitney-type service might more effectively meet the dispersed travel patterns exhibited by the riding public.

A third important aspect of the demonstration projects which was discussed in the Long Island study, concerns the role played by employers and referral agencies. It was shown that attitudes assumed by the Councils might have restricted the full potential of the demonstration projects there. In addition, the attitudes of the unskilled worker in evaluating a low-paying job against the alternative of an equal income which he would receive from public assistance, would also affect the outcome of a demonstration project. This latter factor was not considered in either the Long Island or the Los Angeles study.

In summary, it can be concluded that the results produced by these two demonstration projects have not convincingly supported the validity of the hypothesis that linking poverty areas to job sites would alleviate unemployment among low-income workers. The cause of this weakness was due to the lack of a method for providing desired measures of effectiveness with which to evaluate the objectives of the demonstration projects, rather than the inadequacy of the underlying project concepts.

Even more significant, from a financial viewpoint, is the question of whether or not to undertake a demonstration project in an area. If, for example, the objective of a demonstration is to lower unemployment, then it is important to estimate the projected reduction in unemployment that might be necessary to justify the expenditures. The task to be resolved by the policy-maker is: how much transportation is necessary to achieve a desired level of unemployment reduction. It is with this task that Chapter 5 is concerned.

Other Studies

By 1967, the problems of the transportation needs of low-income neighborhoods became the public concern in many cities. Numerous technical studies were undertaken with the aid of a new program of HUD (U.S. Department of Housing and Urban Development) grants which began in September 1967.[c]

The hypothesis common in all these technical studies was that the availability of transportation access to job opportunities influences the employment status of a member of the labor force. What was generally ignored by these studies, however, was that removing the transportation barrier would in no way insure that every unemployed person will find a job. Indeed there are many other factors as to why a person, able to do work, is not employed. Some of these factors could be identified and consequently interrelated and analyzed. Some factors could be identified but difficult to measure, and others may escape our intellection.

A discussion of these nontransportation causes of unemployment is found in the next two chapters. The point made here concerns the problem that exists whenever one conducts an analysis dealing with the causative effect that one variable may have on another. The case in point is transportation (the causative variable) and unemployment (the dependent variable).

Studies made to analyze the effect of transportation on unemployment have failed to either recognize or to properly measure some of the following effect variables:

1. The distribution of jobs available and compatible to the skill levels of the unemployed.
2. Personal attitudes towards work.
3. Educational attainment of the unemployed.
4. Alternate means of income (i.e., public welfare).
5. Discrimination practices of employers.

The failure to properly account for some of these variables, led to the weak conclusions and findings of the two demonstration projects discussed earlier. A review of the technical studies made in other cities also indicates that implementation of some of the recommended plans[d] may in effect result in similar inconclusive findings regarding the effect of transportation improvements in lowering unemployment.

Measuring the Transportation Variable

Not only did these studies fail to properly account for the nontransportation causes of unemployment, but, even more seriously perhaps, they did not

[c]For example, in 1968, 13 cities received grants: Phoenix, Ariz.; Fresno, Oakland, San Bernardino, and San Jose, Calif.; Denver, Colo.; Chicago, Ill.; Honolulu, Hawaii; Lawrence, Mass.; Omaha, Neb.; Newark, N.J.; Syracuse, N.Y.; and Richmond, Va.

[d]In most cases recommendations for improvement invariably called for additional and/or more frequent transit service to increase the job accessibility potential of the low-income worker. In some cases new lines were recommended to connect job sites that were previously accessible only by automobile.

adequately measure the transportation variable so that its effect on unemployment could be determined.

In a study[6] for the Boston area it was proposed to use an index of measure by calculating the number of jobs reachable in a 30-minute travel time. Transportation systems would then be evaluated on the basis of this criterion (in addition to other criteria) for aiding in the selection of a system which would maximize employment accessibility. This concept is illustrated in Figure 4-1 which shows isochrones of 30 minutes for two systems (1 and 2). In this case, the incremental "benefit" of system 2 may be measured in terms of incremental accessibility to job sites provided by system 2.

This approach is appealing conceptually, and if subject to the constraints of existing and proposed transportation systems, it may well serve the purpose. It is not useful, however, in cases where one seeks to identify the level and quality of transportation systems which are necessary to increase the employment levels among the low-income workers.

This problem is treated later on. The analysis relies primarily on the data collected for the Central Brooklyn Model Cities Area of New York City.

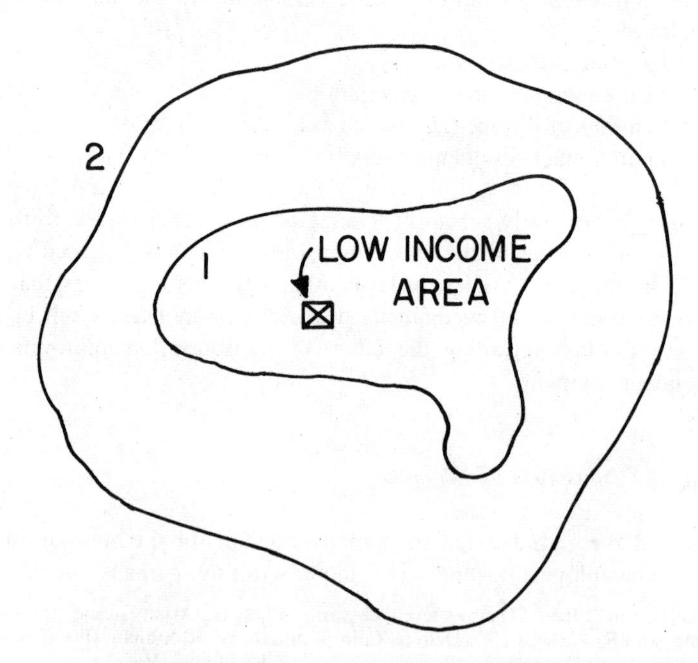

Figure 4-1. Jobs Accessible in 30 Minutes

Projects for the Young

There are few recorded attempts at improving the lot of transit-dependent youth. Only in the area of school busing and transportation for the young handicapped (generally mentally handicapped) are there organized systems which have been developed specifically for the young. For youth in general it is "the thumb or the bus," as it was put succinctly at the Conference on Transportation and Human Needs in the 1970s.[7] Students have organized and operated informal systems at various universities: Maryland and MIT among them. But no officially organized, publicly run, government-financed or underwritten systems have developed. At the University of Wisconsin at Madison, for instance, in the midst of the spirit of "revolution" of the 1960s, a system of "white bikes" was loosely arranged, in which a white-painted bike could be freely picked up, used, and set down anywhere in the city. The bicycles were stolen very rapidly, however. The need to supplement idealism with practicality has subverted many a worthy program for providing better transportation to the disadvantaged.

For school-age handicapped children, on the other hand, there have been the Elementary and Secondary School Amendments of 1969 (Public Law 91-230) which have provided

1. Aid to state-operated or state-supported schools for handicapped children under Title I (Education of Disadvantaged Children).
2. Fifteen percent of funds for the handicapped under Title II (Supplemental Education Centers and Services).
3. Ten percent of funds for handicapped children under the Vocational Education Act.

Evaluation

Those attempts at providing low-cost public transportation for the young are specifically oriented toward school attendance. As necessary transportation, there is no doubt that they are successful. As economic arrangements, no success evaluation can possibly be made of such programs except to compare the most subjective parameters to the most objective: money. Funds applied to the transport of physically or mentally handicapped youngsters likewise must be considered in the light of socially oriented goals.

Since no formal programs have been developed for youth in general, an evaluation is impossible. Again, should such projects be developed they can perhaps not be considered with self-sufficiency as an intent, but must be thought of in terms of overall social programming.

Projects for the Elderly

In general, aside from projects directed entirely at providing links to jobs for the unemployed, it is for the aged, or the aged and handicapped together, that most demonstration projects have been mounted. Generally again, those projects which have been mounted have been of two basic kinds: reduced fare or "minibus." "Reduced fare" refers to a program of allowing patrons, generally elderly or school children to purchase passage for less than the general charge; "minibus" refers to inaugurating a special vehicle for the elderly, usually, but not necessarily, smaller than the usual city bus. A third category is the concept of "dial-a-ride," "demand-actuated" service, which will be discussed later.

Reduced Fares

In the area of reduced fares, usually operating only during nonrush hours, there were thirty-four plans by 1969; over 100 programs by 1972. John Crain listed twenty-eight of the major systems in 1973 (see Table 4-5). The aged pay from 35 to 50 percent of regular fares. Most of the schemes allow usage only during off-peak periods, although recently Chicago extended its program to 24-hour usage. Ridership has increased, on the average, some 15 percent, due to price reductions of about 40 percent.

The best known of these by far are those of Chicago and New York. The New York system reached 800,000 elderly persons (and, incidentally, 2,000,000 school children). By cutting the fare in half, there was a net increase in ridership of some 15-20 percent. But there remained a net loss in revenues, made up by City subsidy.

There are about one million elderly New Yorkers, something over 13 percent of the city's population. Most live independently, and most are capable of using the City's public transit. But in 1969, over half had incomes below $3000; one-third under $2000.

Most of the City's elderly were reached first through banks, then through the 53 Senior Centers and "Little City Halls" maintained at that time.

In the first two-and-a-half years of operation of this program, it cost the City, in subsidies, some $35,000,000, or $25 per person per year.

It was found, however, that the program did affect mobility of the elderly, in that there was an increase in elderly riders (see Table 4-6).

It did not, however, necessarily reach those who should, theoretically, benefit most from such a program. The level of registration for the program was highest in predominantly white areas (see Table 4-7).

An interesting result of studies of this program was the breakdown by trip purpose (see Table 4-8).

In Chicago, older people were reached through group services, public housing,

Table 4-5
Cities Known to Have Reduced Fare Plans for Older Persons

State	Cities	State	Cities
California:	Los Angeles San Diego San Francisco	New Mexico:	Albuquerque
		New York:	Merrick New York
Connecticut:	Hartford Meriden New Haven Stamford	Ohio:	Ashtabula Cleveland Toledo
Illinois:	Chicago	Pennsylvania:	Philadelphia
Indiana:	Terre Haute	Rhode Island:	Pawtucket Providence
Iowa:	Cedar Rapids Davenport Des Moines	Washington:	Seattle Tacoma
Massachusetts:	Boston	West Virginia:	Clarksburg
Michigan:	Detroit Flint Grand Rapids		

Source: Crain, J.L. "The Transportation Problems of Transit Dependent Persons–A Status Report," in *Conference on Transportation and Human Needs–The Second Phase*, June 1973, American University, Washington, D.C., Table 3.

community centers, and the like. A sample of the ridership found a breakdown of 32 percent male, 68 percent female, of which about 7 percent were employed, 81 percent were in "good" health, 9 percent in "excellent" health, and 10 percent in "poor" health. It was found that 75 percent uses buses, 10 percent rapid transit, 11 percent auto, 3 percent taxi, and 1 percent railroad. Factors in their selection of mode involved *convenience* (59 to 70 percent); *cost* (12 to 32 percent); and *health* (10 to 17 percent).

Overall, fare reductions resulted in an 86 percent increase in the number of trips made by senior citizens.

But the increase in riders again was not enough to prevent a net loss to the Chicago Transit Authority.

Table 4-6
Increase in Elderly Riders by Borough and City, New York City 1969

Area	Samples: Before People	Samples: Before Hours	Samples: After People	Samples: After Hours	People per Bus per Hour: Before	After	Change	% Change
Brooklyn	448	31.4	484	28.7	14.3	16.9	+2.6	+18.2
Queens	243	25.1	365	33.5	9.7	10.9	+1.2	+12.4
Manhattan	424	50.5	504	41.0	8.4	12.3	+3.9	+46.4
Bronx	146	15.0	207	15.0	9.8	13.8	+4.0	+40.9
Richmond	15	4.1	29	5.5	3.7	5.3	+1.6	+43.3
Total	1276	126.1	1589	123.7	10.1	12.8	+2.7	+26.7

Source: Cantor, M.H., "The Reduced Fare Program for New Yorkers," in Cantilli, E.J., and Shmelzer, J.L., (eds.) *Transportation and Aging–Selected Issues*, U.S. Department of Health, Education, and Welfare, Washington, D.C., 1970.

Table 4-7
Level of Reduced Fare Registration in White and Nonwhite Health Areas Located Within Poverty Areas[a] [Brooklyn, 1970 (in percent)]

Level of Registration[b]	Health Areas: Nonwhite	White[c]	Nonwhite	White
Low	53.6	6.9	0	0
Medium	39.3	51.8	0	31.8
High	7.1	41.3	0	68.2
Total	100.0	100.0	0	100.0

[a]A health area is classified as within a poverty area if at least half is located in a poverty area as designated by the Human Resources Administration.

[b]Level of registration was obtained by comparing the number of registrants per health area with the City Planning Commission. Estimates (1965) of the elderly population of that health area. Low registration is defined as 0-19 percent, medium registration as 20-39, and high as 40 percent and over.

[c]Level of density of white elderly is based on Planning Commission estimates (1965). A health area is designated as nonwhite if less than 50 percent of its elderly population is white; a white health area has 50 percent or more white population.

Source: Cantor, M.H., "The Reduced Fare Program for Older New Yorkers," in Cantilli, E.J. and Shmelzer, J.L. (eds.), *Transportation and Aging–Selected Issues*, U.S. Department of Health, Education, and Welfare, Washington, D.C., 1970.

Table 4-8
Rank Order Frequency of Older Persons' Trip Purposes Before and After Introduction of a Reduced Fare Plan, New York City, June and August, 1969[a]

Purpose	Before	After
Social contact[b]	33%	31%
Shopping[c]	31%	31%
Medical[d]	22%	18%
Other	12%	13%
Business	11%	10%
Medical supplies	5%	3%
Social services	3%	3%
Religious	2%	1%

[a]Based on percent of total trips; totals add to more than 100 percent since some trips were for multiple purposes.

[b]Includes: visiting, recreation, and trips to day centers.

[c]Includes food and other shopping.

[d]Includes visits to doctors and clinics.

Source: Cantor, M.H., "The Reduced Fare Program for Older New Yorkers," in Cantilli, E.J., and Shmelzer, J.L. (eds.) *Transportation and Aging–Selected Issues*, U.S. Department of Health, Education, and Welfare, Washington, D.C., 1970.

"Minibuses"

In the "minibus" area, there have been experiments such as those in Prince Georges County, Maryland, where six sixty-passenger buses (hardly "mini," but special in concept) were used in transporting senior citizens to clubs and centers, generally on Mondays through Saturdays, at a fee of 35 cents; the Emmett, Idaho, "Senior Citizen A-Go-Go," a government-surplus bus and a used school-bus, used for field trips to "interesting places"; and the Chicago YMCA Senior Citizen Mobile Service, for trips to health centers, welfare agencies, shopping tours, and social outings.[10]

One of the first real "minibus" operations was the YMCA Senior Citizens Mobile Service, in Chicago, which was financed by the U.S. Department of Health, Education, and Welfare, and ran from September 1966 through November 1969. The YMCA of Metropolitan Chicago developed this service, which began with two seven-passenger vans, to dissipate the immobility of many senior citizens, which, it was felt, leads to loneliness from isolation, and frustration from hunger and pain. This was one of the first "dial-a-ride" arrangements, also, in that patrons called the mobile service office for transportation, and were placed on the schedule on a first-call-first-served basis. The schedule was made up a day in advance.

During the three-year demonstration period, the service carried a total of 1,606 senior citizens on more than 30,403 trips, at a cost of about $32,000. A picture of the development of the service can be seen in Figure 4-2, showing the number of requests per month for the project. Drops in use during the generally upward trend are attributed to snowstorms, cold weather, and summer months when programs are curtailed.[11]

Another project in this classification was that of Cape May, New Jersey, operating in 1968 and 1969. In this case a 9-passenger Volkswagen bus was used in a service for senior citizens, at a cost of $13,927 (to the state and the city of Cape May) for its first year of operation. With fares of from 25 to 75 cents per trip, it carried some 8,300 passengers in 20 months of service.[12]

And yet another "minibus" operation was that of "Little House," a multipurpose center for the elderly in Menlo Park, California. In 1969 the sponsoring (volunteer) organization bought a 12-passenger Ford Econoline bus for transporting the elderly to and from the center.

This system began with fixed routes and scheduled stops, but this kind of system did not meet the needs of the riders. A more flexible operation was developed with "corridors" of scheduled movement and home pickup based on phone-ins or standing reservations. In this case it is Little House members, the elderly themselves, who drive the vehicle. About 500 riders a month were using this system in 1970. It was estimated that the cost was about 60 cents per person per ride.[13]

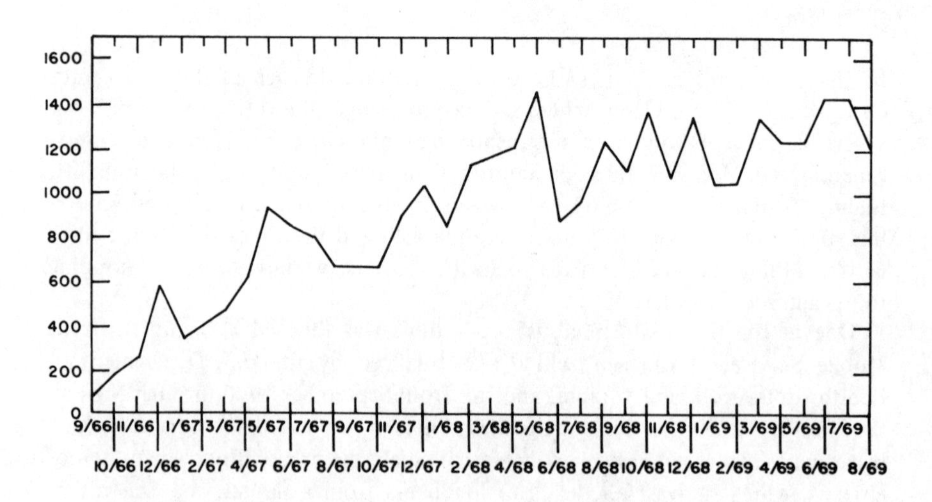

Figure 4-2. Senior Citizens Mobile Service: Monthly Transportation Participation Record, September 1966 to October 1969. Source: Bell, J.H., "Senior Citizens Mobile Service," in Cantilli, E.J., and Shmelzer, J.L. (eds.), *Transportation and Aging–Selected Issues*, U.S. Department of Health, Education, and Welfare, Washington, D.C. 1970.

"Dial-A-Ride" and "Door-to-Door"

"Dial-A-Ride" is a third grouping of types of improvements for the aged (and others), although it may very well include elements of the other two: it may use "minibuses," and it may offer reduced fares. Dial-A-Ride, or "door-to-door" service, may refer to being picked up, at your door, either in relation to a fixed-route system or a "demand-responsive" system. Figure 4-3 shows user locations in relation to a fixed-route system; Figure 4-4 shows the demand-responsive system.

The Haddonfield, New Jersey, dial-a-ride program is perhaps the most famous. It began operations in March 1972, and has had as much as 17 percent of its ridership classifiable as "elderly." The system utilizes eleven buses on regular routing, plus one specially designed bus capable of accommodating wheelchairs. The system operates within an area of five square miles, with all requests for service coming into a central control center. With each bus carrying its own radio receiver transmitter, routing can be adapted immediately to telephoned requests.[15]

Cranston, Rhode Island, has instituted a dial-a-ride system directed at the elderly and the handicapped, specifically oriented toward trips to hospitals and doctors. Four buses are used, three regular buses and one especially equipped to handle the handicapped. One day's notice is required for service.[16]

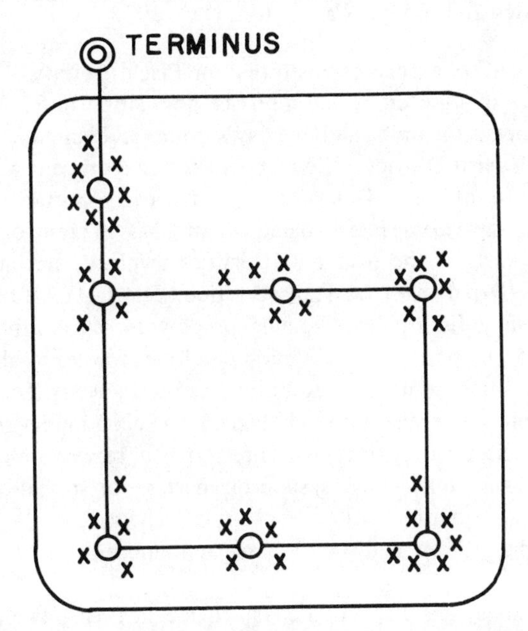

Figure 4-3. User Locations Related to Fixed-Route Service. Source: "Dial-A-Bus Guidelines for Design and Implementation," in *Demand-Responsive Transportation Systems*, Special Report 136, Highway Research Board, Washington, D.C., 1973.

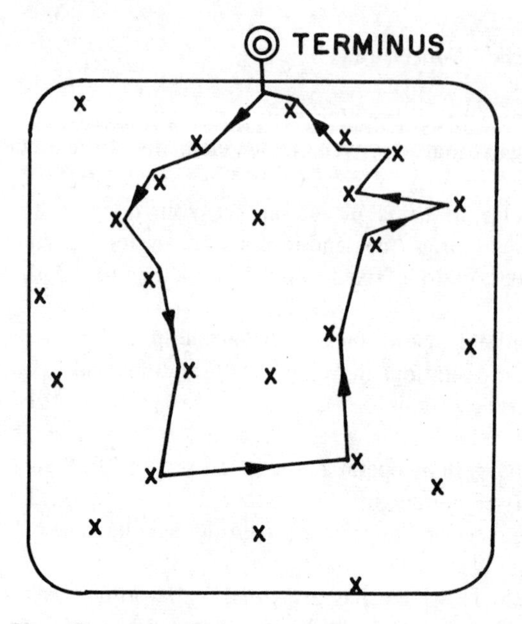

Figure 4-4. User Locations Related to Demand-Responsive Service. Source: "Dial-A-Bus Guidelines for Design and Implementation," in *Demand-Responsive Transportation Systems*, Special Report 136, Highway Research Board, Washington, D.C., 1973

This is similar to a scheme instituted in Placid County, California, in an urban-rural area of nine cities and a service population of 77,000. In this case there are four operating units, and one day's notice is required.[17]

The Valley Transit District in Connecticut is an experiment which combines a number of points of view. This project provides transportation for clients of health and social service agencies, based on an UMTA[e] grant of $384,000, plus $10,000 from each of the four municipalities involved, and another $26,000 from the State Department of Transportation. The UMTA funds can only be used for routing, dispatching, training employees, establishing the district, engineering and purchasing specially modified buses for use by the handicapped, six in all. State funds are used for additional hardware needs. The attempt in this project is to confront physical, psychological, and economic barriers met by the elderly and handicapped in traveling. Three types of service are offered: normal, scheduled routes; a "rent-a-bus" system of charters for special occasions; and a door-to-door service reminiscent of "dial-a-ride" schemes.

Fares are charged on a distance basis, and monthly bills may be sent to participants.[18]

Tucson, Arizona, has also initiated a scheme involving twenty vans, ten of which are specifically for the handicapped, ten for door-to-door service, at a cost of $500,000.[19]

[e]Urban Mass Transportation Administration of the U.S. Department of Transportation.

Model Cities Program funds have been used in some cases, as in Seattle, Washington (to the tune of $300,000), for the institution of special bus runs, but generally for low-income groups not necessarily elderly.[20]

Two of the most recent demonstration programs directed at mobility of the elderly took place in the New York Metropolitan Area. The first, in East Orange, New Jersey, was a marked departure from any of the projects described above. The second was a dial-a-ride program, with a difference.

East Orange, New Jersey, Mobility Project

East Orange is a city of 75,000 just west of Newark, New Jersey, across the Hudson River (about 20 miles) from New York City. It is unique in that it has an aged population of 13,000, constituting some 17 percent of the total population of the city. And while 53 percent of the city's population is black, most of the elderly are white, at a ratio of four to one.

The elderly are dispersed throughout the city, in low- and middle-income senior citizens' housing, in boarding homes, hotels, and apartments. About 30 percent live alone.

The basic premise for this demonstration project grew out of the Conference/Workshop on Transportation and Aging of 1970. It was suggested that it might be helpful to the elderly to provide "an escort service, or transportation aides to accompany an elderly person who is making trips within a city." It was hoped that this service would effectively increase the senior citizen's mobility.

Accordingly a service was organized providing a traveling companion for any length of trip, utilizing public transportation. Ostensibly, public transportation in East Orange is more than adequate, with four stations of the Erie Lackawanna Railroad, offering intra- and inter-state service, and twenty-one bus routes within the city. In addition there are a number of taxi stands in the city.

Another reason for choosing East Orange for this project was the community's awareness and concern. The City government has a Senior Citizen's Activity Department, and there are numerous programs for the elderly sponsored by churches and other groups.

The original concept of this escort service envisioned the use of volunteers as escorts, but this did not work out. Escorts were hired, generally from among middle-aged ladies, and even to some degree among the elderly themselves.

During a year of operation, five escorted bus trips, thirty-one escorted taxicab trips, and twenty-four escorted walking trips were made. There are many apparent and real reasons for this lack of patronage for a free escort service, discussed later (see Evaluation).[21]

Bronx, New York, Dial-A-Ride

This dial-a-ride project took place in the Bronx, New York, the northern borough of the city of New York. A portion of that borough was delineated as containing a high proportion of elderly residents. In this case, these are the elderly "left behind," mostly immigrant ethnic groups, as children move away to the suburbs.

The difference in this dial-a-ride project was in the use of existing car service vehicles, rather than in the provision of "minibuses" or other bus vehicles. In the city of New York, local law distinguishes between regulated "taxicabs," which measure fares by meter, and "car service" or "livery car" arrangements, which can only respond to telephone calls. The organization of the Bronx dial-a-ride program involved use of these "livery cars" on a special basis, and reduced rates, for the elderly.

To design the system, surveys were performed to estimate anticipated demand for the service. Of the respondents, 71 percent stated that dial-a-ride service was needed in their area. Table 4-9 shows that those reporting infirmities thought it a better idea than those that did not, by a slight margin.

It was conservatively estimated that five percent of the apparent 71 percent of those favorable would actually use the system. This came to 2000 persons, roughly equal to 10 percent of the elderly population in the area.

A study of costs resulted in establishment of fares at 75 cents per person per trip for cab trips carrying one or two passengers, and 50 cents per person per trip for groups of three persons or more.

Throughout the first six months of operation, Dial-A-Ride attracted no more than 65 person-trips per week. This contrasted markedly with a projected 1190 person trips per week in the planning phase. Group riding did not materialize, and overall demand was low. In addition, the cost per trip levelled off at $1.20, causing a loss to the operator.

In a second phase of this demonstration, fares were uniformly reduced to 50 cents, with the difference in cost made up as a subsidy to the operator. In this phase service was made available seven days a week, twenty-four hours a day. The ridership figures which resulted are seen in Table 4-10.

Comparing these results with previous projections, the project produced about 10 percent of expected demand. Ridership rose at the beginning of the project, and fell at the end. Its peak was achieved in the middle (May).[22]

Table 4-9
Opinion of Need for Dial-a-Ride

	Yes	No	No Response
All respondents	71%	4%	25%
Those reporting infirmities	76%	3%	20%
Those not reporting infirmities	67%	5%	28%

Table 4-10
Summary of Weekly Ridership on Dial-a-Ride, by Month—Second Phase

Month	Weekdays Only	Weekend Only	7-Day Week
March	196	38	237
April	314	42	337
May	310	36	355
June	240	25	271
July	305	7	295
August	134	7	146
Average	250	22	274

Projects for the Rural Elderly

The rural elderly are perhaps a special group within this overall area of demonstration. Because they are a minority within a minority (most elderly, as do most citizens, reside in urban areas), demonstration projects, and, indeed, concern, are sparser. An OEO demonstration project, however, was conducted in Raleigh County, West Virginia, to provide transportation for the rural poor. The area is central Appalachia, and with no jobs available in the vicinity, the provision of transportation could not help to provide employment.

The project started in 1967 and was funded (a total of $151,464) for 19 months. Eight-passenger Chevrolet carryalls were used, generally operating above capacity (nine or ten persons), with the average round trip at three hours, covering 45 miles. Costs for the project came to about $64,000 per year, and for an estimated 250 persons per year this came to $256 per person per year, or $178 per person per year for an ongoing system similar to the demonstration project.[23]

Important changes were made in the travel patterns of people who used the free bus. The saving of money is the obvious one, but the distribution of trips by purpose changed to a marked degree. Trips for community action and shopping increased most, with trips for church, food stamps, and medical staying the same.

Those who used the OEO bus traveled more than they did before, but only by 5 percent. However, people made more multipurpose trips than they did before.[24]

Evaluation

The reduced-fares projects can all be called eminently successful, except that they result in costing a good deal of money. Such projects have certainly demonstrated a resulting increase in *usage* of public transit by the elderly. This can reasonably be interpreted as an increase in *mobility*, since we can assume that the increases are in trips which would not have been made. The increases, however, do not meet or exceed that number which would obviate a need for subsidy. The decision, therefore, of "success" in these programs cannot lie in a purely economic interpretation. But the logic of subsidizing transportation for any group within the general population must be considered: are the elderly subsidized because they are elderly or because they are (generally) poor? If it is done as a "reward" for being elderly it is one argument. If as a help to limited income, then the justification must be extended to all those of limited income. Our human difficulties in applying reason equitably must be challenged and our actions must be questioned. The elderly are a special group not because of arbitrary age thresholds but because of either physical or mental abnormalities, or because of economic inadequacy, or both. If our self-admitted reason for providing a service is the former, then the reasoning must extend to other physically or mentally disabled persons. In this case we have developed schemes for the handicapped, but rarely do they extend to lowered fares. If, on the other hand, our reason is the latter, then we should review the transportation needs of other segments of the poverty-level population.

In similar vein, it may be said that all "minibus" projects were successful if they carried even one elderly person. But while half-fare programs' deficits can be absorbed into big-city general-fund budgets, special-vehicle projects have usually been saddled with a need, whether justified or not, to demonstrate self-sufficiency. Indeed, this is often the intent of federally sponsored program development. But like public transit everywhere, it is difficult to find one which turns a profit or even breaks even.

Most "minibus" projects have been more or less informal arrangements supported by volunteer organizations. In such cases a return on an investment is not a prime requisite, and, indeed, the venture is not considered as an investment. Therefore, whether a fare is charged or not is not of prime consequence in such a case, and the service continues only as long as funds can be diverted to the project.

The Chicago YMCA minibus operation for instance, underwritten by the U.S. Department of Health, Education, and Welfare, made no attempt at self-sufficiency, providing a service at a total cost of about 60 cents per mile during the period September 1966 to June 1969. The cost analysis is seen in Table 4-11.[25]

The Cape May project had economic problems in trying to become self-sufficient. In 1970 it operated at a deficit of $18,000, with no significant increase in income over the $2,004.50 collected in fares. In fact the comparison of $2,004.50 in income versus $20,463.00 in expenditure is, in miniature, the problem of mass transit in this country. Maintenance became a prime headache for this small service, and without subsidy such activities cannot continue.[26]

The service offered by "Little House" is at a cost of 60 cents a ride, quite

Table 4-11
Cost Analysis–Chicago YMCA Minibus (Table 4-11 presents a cost analysis of a single mobile unit over the period September 1966 to June 15, 1969.)

Operating Expense:		
Gasoline and oil		$2,168.80
Repairs		1,828.96
Wash		43.83
Licenses		108.90
Insurance		760.00
Parking		3.50
Depreciation:		
Cost 8/22/66, Dodge 7 passenger van	$2,442.00	
Less estimated salvage value	342.00	
Depreciable cost	$2,100.00	
Estimated useful life of mobile unit – 3 years @ $700 per year		2,100.00
Total Operation Expense		$7,013.99

Number of miles driven, September 1966–June 15, 1969	53,132	
Operating cost, per mile	0.1320¢	
Salaries:		
Mobile Unit Drivers		$13,411.26
Office Dispatcher (75% of Salary)		10,755.00
Total Salaries–Driver and Dispatcher		$24,166.26
Salary cost, per mile	0.4548¢	
Total operating, Driver and Dispatcher expense per mile	0.5868¢	

Notes: Total gross salaries were used. Fringe benefits were not included in the figures. Fringe benefits would include group insurance and hospitalization. As many as three drivers were used at one period with the drivers working in shifts. At present there is only one driver on a full time basis.

Source: Bell, J.H., "Senior Citizens Mobile Service," in Cantilli, E.J., and Shmelzer, J.L. (eds.) *Transportation and Aging–Selected Issues*, U.S. Department of Health, Education, and Welfare, Washington, D.C., 1970.

comparable to the costs incurred in Chicago, but quite closer to a bearable figure (as a fare) than the costs incurred in Cape May (at over 2 dollars a ride). Again, however, the Little House venture was sponsored by a volunteer group, and it may be that additional costs were absorbed which are not considered unless an operation must account for its expenditures.[27]

As of August, 1972, the Haddonfield operation carried more than 3000 one-way trips per week, and 500 to 600 per day, with usage increasing. It was noted that there was high usage during nonpeak, nonwork trips.[28]

In Bay Ridges, Ontario, only 50 percent of costs could be covered by revenue. The cost per trip was variable, from 50 cents to $1.36, averaging at 55 cents.[29]

The "B-Line Dial-A-Bus" system, of Batavia, N.Y., saw its ridership increase from 944 to 1500 after five weeks, and to 2000 in sixteen weeks. In this case all operating expenses have been covered by revenues.[30]

Interesting user responses to the Ann Arbor system are shown in Table 4-12.

The dial-a-ride approach is being tested in England, in Abingdon, Bristol, Harlow New Town, Chelmsford, and Harrogate, among other locations. One problem which has emerged is the lower distribution of telephones in England as opposed to the U.S., telephones being found in only 40 percent of households in England.[31]

A summary of the characteristics of some prominent demand-responsive systems is given in Table 4-13. The performance of these same systems is compared in Table 4-14. It is noteworthy that the Haddonfield system is the most expensive. There were no major attempts to reduce costs, since it is a federally financed demonstration project. But costs for demand-responsive

Table 4-12
Responses Regarding User's Experience with Service

Response	Respondents (percent)
Totally dissatisfied and will not use again	3.9
Neutral or supportive but automobile satisfies travel needs and cannot perceive of any possible future need for service	18.6
Only moderately dissatisfied or supportive and might use again under extreme circumstances, i.e., if automobile is disabled	15.7
Dissatisfied with service but use on irregular basis	0.0
Satisfied with service and use on irregular basis	52.0
Satisfied and use regularly	8.8
No response	1.0

Source: Urbanik, T., II, "Dial-A-Ride Project in Ann Arbor: Description and Operation," in *Demand-Responsive Transportation Systems*, Special Report 136, Highway Research Board, Washington, D.C. 1973

Table 4-13
Characteristics of Demand-Responsive Transportation Systems

	Population Served	Square Miles Served	Service Hours	Peak Hour	Number of Vehicles Midday	Other
Ann Arbor, Michigan	17,000	2.4	6:30A.M.-6:00P.M.	3	2	
Batavia, New York	17,300	4.75	6:00A.M.-6:00P.M.	5	3	
Bay Ridges, Ontario	13,700	1.34	5:00A.M.-1:00A.M.	5	3	
Columbus, Ohio	55,000	2.5	6:00A.M.-9:30P.M.	4	3	2
Haddonfield, New Jersey	27,500	8.1	Continuous	11	5	1
Regina, Saskatchewan	35,000	5.5	6:45A.M.-11:35P.M.	10		

Source: Roos, D., "Doorstep Transit," in *Environment*, June 1974, Table 1.

Table 4-14
System Performance

	Average Daily Patronage	Average Passengers/ Vehicle Hour	Average Service Demands/Square Mile/Hour	Average Cost/ Vehicle Hour	Average Cost/ Passenger
Ann Arbor, Michigan	200	6.0	7	$14.60	$1.74
Batavia, New York	340	13.0	6	$12.50	$0.92
Bay Ridges, Ontario	700	17.0	30	$ 8.45	$0.60
Columbus, Ohio	355	8.4	9	$16.06	$1.53
Haddonfield, New Jersey	730	6.1	4	$15.40	$2.48
Regina, Saskatchewan	2,000	20	21	$13.43	$0.71

Source: Roos, D., "Doorstep Transit," in *Environment*, June 1974, Table 2.

systems are not low, and if it is desirable to charge low fares (as is the case when the system is for the disadvantaged), then deficits are inevitable.[32]

The East Orange experiment in providing escorts for elderly citizens' aid on public transportation may be termed an abysmal failure outright, or the conditions and circumstances under which the project took place can be analyzed, and the outcome scrutinized for lessons applicable to future attempts. For instance, while it had appeared that the city was well-covered by public transit (basically buses), the start of the demonstration program unfortunately coincided with the first of a series of bus strikes. Even after the strikes had ended, normal service was not resumed. Bus trips had been the least common form of travel for that segment of the elderly population which was expected to use the escort service; after the strikes it became even less important and desirable to these people.

From another standpoint, it appeared that such a service can only be ancillary to some more basic service, such as transportation itself. There was widespread misunderstanding among the elderly contacted that the service offered involved an escort *and a vehicle* of some kind. Those who use public transportation without an escort obviously find no physical need for an escort; those who do not would require a great deal of psychological support to use a facility they felt insecure about.

Of the few persons who did use the service, it is noteworthy that most trips were by taxicabs, evenly divided between shopping and medical purposes; and the remainder were walking trips, most of which were for shopping.

The majority of users had incomes of less than $200.00 per month, half of them with physical handicaps, and with a usual "life-space" encompassing only the general proximity of their residences.

A survey made near the conclusion of the project, to help determine the reasons behind the poor usage of the service, found that:

1. Few of the respondents (who had not utilized the service) saw any need for it.
2. Few of the respondents could think of anyone else who might need it.
3. Most respondents had someone they could turn to if help was needed.
4. Most respondents had friends and/or relatives living nearby.
5. Many respondents saw more need for a vehicle to go with the service.

It would appear that the escort service concept was not applicable to the situation of East Orange, New Jersey, at the time it was introduced. It would also appear that if any conclusion should be drawn about this experience, it is that:

1. An escort service should be directed at low-income, physically handicapped elderly.
2. The service should be part of another program offering a service to the elderly.
3. Cost is a real barrier to the use of public transportation by the elderly, with or without an escort.
4. An escort service has more potential as an adjunct to more personalized transportation services, i.e., "door-to-door," or "dial-a-ride," than being tied to public transportation.[33]

The Bronx dial-a-ride project seemed also to miss its projected mark by a considerable distance. But again, a review of the conditions under which it operated is edifying. During both phases of the program's operation (described earlier), the service was operated as a door-to-door system. To develop a steady clientele, the project staff attempted to generate agreements with several organizations located in the general area, as to transporting their elderly or handicapped clients to and from their centers. These efforts did not succeed. The primary source of dial-a-ride customers became, instead, persons who used the service only occasionally. In fact, only 10 percent of users made about 50 percent of the trips. This small number formed the basis of the patronage of the system. By contrast, the more successful dial-a-ride programs have had a large percentage of regular subscribers. In fact, it is apparent that the more successful projects provide some form of subscription service.

Regular subscribers to dial-a-ride systems tend to have common destinations or origins, making it possible to increase vehicle productivity. The Bronx dial-a-ride system, without regular subscribers, did not have a reasonable chance of success. System productivity reached a level of only three trips per vehicle-hour. This compares most unfavorably to other systems (see Table 4-15). Even with fare subsidy, the operator was not able to gross $6.50 per hour, which had been determined to be a minimum acceptable figure. This made the operator reluctant to reserve vehicles for exclusive dial-a-ride use, and in fact made dial-a-ride secondary to the operator's usual customer service. This attitude was expressed to the elderly through the operator not answering telephones, not providing on-time pickup, and a general lack of commitment by drivers, operators, and dispatchers.

The results of this experiment were not conclusive, since so much resulted from attitudes. It may be that the ultimate recommendation to be made is that such a service must have its own staff, its own vehicles (probably larger and more comfortable than normal passenger cars), and (unless totally volunteer-staffed) a guaranteed hourly revenue to workers.[34]

The rural free bus system in Raleigh County was assessed at an overall benefit of $91,563 (see Table 4-16).

It is apparent that transportation programs in rural areas can stimulate economic development, and can affect the *employability* of persons even if no jobs exist immediately. In addition, they can affect social and political awareness and life styles (the "life space" concept) by providing access to opportunities.

However, commercial buses in the area naturally lost money, and such a consideration must be entered in the balances of evaluation.[35]

Projects for the Handicapped

Projects specifically designed for the handicapped have not been common, except for handicapped or retarded children or similar groups. The "minibus" or

Table 4-15
Dial-A-Ride System Productivity

Test Area	Trips/Vehicle Hour
Ann Arbor	8
Columbus, Ohio	7
Toronto	13
Regina (Canada)	15
Columbia, Md.	6
Batavia, N.Y.	10

Source: Crain, J.L., "The Transportation Problem of Transit Dependent Persons–A Status Report," in *Conference on Transportation and Human Needs–The Second Phase*, June 1973, American University, Washington, D.C., Table 4.

Table 4-16
Annual Benefits and Disbenefits of the Free Bus System in Raleigh County

Impact Group and Specific Impact	Direct Effects, Dollars		Value Added Through Multiplier Effects, Dollars[a]	
	Benefit	Disbenefit	Benefit	Disbenefit
Transportation system users–transportation savings	26,880		6,470	
Income from government programs	24,481		5,849	
Income effect of shopping opportunities	7,680			
Imputed válue of transportation	6,252			
Imputed value of health care	1,600			
Transport service providers: free bus employees–salaries	28,899		6,935	
Transport service providers: suppliers of free bus–profit on vehicles	700		163	
Profits and wages for maintenance service	3,174		762	
Material value added for maintenance			1,904	
Transport service providers: ad hoc operators–loss of income from free bus users		26,004		6,241
Transport service providers: commercial buses–loss of profit from free bus users		44		11
Loss of wages from free bus users		435		104
Loss of material value added				78

Table 4-16 (cont.)

Impact Group and Specific Impact	Direct Effects, Dollars		Value Added Through Multiplier Effects, Dollars[a]	
	Benefit	Disbenefit	Benefit	Disbenefit
Other entrepreneurs: Beckley store owners– change in income as a result of accessibility changes for the poor	18,000		4,320	
Change in income as a result of income effects to the poor	1,536		268	
Change in material value added			11,722	
Other entrepreneurs: rural store owners– change in income as a result of accessibility changes for the poor		18,000		4,320
Change in material value added				10,800
Subtotals	119,202	44,483	38,398	21,554
Net effects	74,719		16,844	
Overall net benefits	91,563			

[a]Value added is calculated by considering the expenditure multiplier effect of the returns to labor and entrepreneurs, in the form of wages and profit.

Source: Burkhardt, J.E., "Transportation and the Rural Elderly," in Cantilli, E.J., and Shmelzer, J.L. (eds.), *Transportation and Aging–Selected Issues*, U.S. Department of Health, Education and Welfare, Washington, D.C., 1970.

"dial-a-ride" projects have been directed at the elderly, or at the "elderly and handicapped" as a group. The Haddonfield, New Jersey, system, for instance, has one special vehicle to provide for wheelchairs; the Cranston, Rhode Island, system provides for "handicapped and elderly"; and Valley Transit has six modified buses for the convenience of the handicapped.

Reduced-fare projects have not included the handicapped as a group as yet, perhaps becuase of the attitude that the handicapped are children, breadwinners, housewives, and the elderly, the poor and the comfortably well off, and a reduced fare is not appropriate to such a group.

Evaluation

Again, wherever vehicles adapted to the use of the handicapped are introduced, they are utilized. Costs are the disputed factor; disputed only insofar as their relative importance to the goal of the project is concerned.

5 Improving Employment Opportunities

Many factors determine whether or not a low-income worker will be employed. For the purpose of this discussion they will be divided into two groups: Those factors which are not transportation-related, and those in which transportation is a determining force.

In this chapter, the analysis of transportation factors is developed formally through the employment-accessibility model. The nontransportation factors, however, are also examined, to place the transportation element in its proper position relative to those other factors which bear on the employment characteristics of the low-income worker.

Factors Affecting the Employment of the Poor

The factors which inhibit employment can be separated into two sets: one which includes elements rooted within the individual (*endogenous* factors), and another which includes elements that are external, and over which the individual has no direct control (*exogenous* factors). Examples of each group are illustrated in Table 5-1.

"Endogenous" Factors

Education, Skill Levels, and Work Habits

Unemployment has its greatest effect on blue-collar and service workers.[1] Of these, the largest proportion of unemployed are individuals who possess no basic skills. Since skill levels are highly correlated to education, one effective method

Table 5-1
Factors Affecting Employability of the Poor

Endogenous Factors	Exogenous Factors
Education	Employer's attitudes
Skill levels	Low wages
Work habits	Welfare institution
	Location factors

of reducing unemployment among the unskilled labor force is through intensive training programs.

The need for training individuals who, because they have little or no education, qualify only for menial or dead-end jobs, has been recognized at all levels of governments. The federal government has taken a lead in this endeavor. Its efforts to increase the employability of jobless and underemployed workers began under the Area Redevelopment Act of 1961 and the Manpower Development and Training Act of 1962.[2] A summary of these federally assisted programs is given in Table 5-2.

These programs are geared to local employment requirements and opportunities and include a wide diversity of occupational objectives, as shown in Table 5-3.

But the process of educating the unskilled entails more than the acquisition of new skills. The trainee must also relate to his prospective employer by meeting work schedules, on-time performance, and the like. "Tardiness," "high degree of absenteeism," and "short employment periods," were the most commonly used terms of employers in the Los Angeles and Long Island demonstration areas, in describing their problems in hiring and retaining unskilled workers.

The "Manpower Report to the President" (1971) noted that from the early 1960s until recently, efforts aimed at alleviating unskilled unemployment had been concentrated on changing the *attitudes* of potential employees. In the past few years, however, the emphasis has shifted from preemployment training to immediate job placement, with the provision of on-the-job supportive services. The success of this approach depends on the willingness of private employers to cooperate.

"Exogenous" Factors

Employer's Attitudes

In 1967, the National Alliance of Businessmen[3] (NAB) made a commitment to hire 100,000 hard-core unemployed persons with emphasis on the *immediate hiring*, coupled with providing supportive services after employment. Most large-scale hiring efforts such as this one, however, have focused on fitting men to existing slots, rather than on changing the environment to better suit previously excluded workers.[4] Morgan's paper suggests, however, that "organizational change" is needed in the implementation of hiring programs."

A report[5] of the JOBS NOW program in Chicago, which supports Morgan's contention, found that a high level of organizational commitments was critical for success of this program.

The type of support which is needed must have a serious commitment to the

Table 5-2

First-Time Enrollments in Federally Assisted Work and Training Programs, Fiscal Year 1964 and 1969-1972 (thousands)

Program	Fiscal Year				
	1964	1969	1970	1971 (Estimated)	1972 (Estimated)
Total	278	1,745	1,819	2,027	2,194
Institutional training under the MDTA	69	135	130	130	
JOBS (federally financed) and other on-the-job training	9	136	178	226	
Neighborhood Youth Corps:					
In school and summer		430	436	311	
Out of school		74	46	64	1,205
Operation Mainstream		11	13	12	
Public service careers		4	4	39	
Concentrated employment program		127	112	113	
Job Corps		53	43	45	
Work Incentive Program		81	93	125	187
Veterans programs		59	83	115	120
Vocational rehabilitation	179	368	411	442	385
Other programs	21	267	271	304	297

Source: *Manpower Report to the President*, April 1971.

Table 5-3
Occupational Distribution of Enrollees in Selected Manpower Programs (percent distribution)

Occupational Group	MDTA Institutional	MDTA On The Job	JOBS	CEP	WIN
Total: Number	130,000	91,000	97,200	25,500	5,700
Percent	100.0	100.0	100.0	100.0	100.0
Professional, technical and managerial	4.5	5.8	3.6	4.0	7.1
Clerical and sales	20.2	12.8	16.1	19.8	23.2
Service	29.5	19.7	7.3	18.1	21.4
Farming, fishing, and forestry	4.9	4.2	.9	1.8	1.7
Processing trades	4.6	5.0	15.5	8.1	5.6
Machine trades	9.3	19.5	16.9	7.9	5.3
Benchwork	8.0	9.3	12.5	11.3	7.2
Structural work	10.7	3.6	11.3	18.2	14.7

Source: *Manpower Report to the President*, April 1971.

program by management *and* by lower-level employees. An example of this is found in the success achieved by IBM, which, in 1968, located a computer component assembly plant in New York City's Bedford-Stuyvesant section.[6] The plant assembles and repairs two products: external computer cables, and power packs for keypunch and verifier machines. In general the jobs are repetitious and low-skilled, a reflection of the current limited scope of the plant. "The work, however, is dignified, and far from the tedious and demeaning jobs many unskilled ghetto employees often receive. These are not dead-end jobs, since there is clear advancement potential in the IBM system and the heavy local hiring gives the residents a real stake in the success of the plant."[7]

IBM's experiment was conceived and supported by Thomas J. Watson, Jr., Chairman of the Board of IBM. IBM became deeply committed to exploring the feasibility of the ability of major industrial companies to set up business in ghetto areas *using local labor.* Because IBM became totally committed to achieving success, the policies it adopted typically reflect the type of organizational reorientation which is needed to relate to special ghetto conditions:

1. It offers its own educational upgrading courses.
2. It encourages its employees to pursue study at accredited academic institutions by refunding 75 percent of tuition fees.
3. It allows employees, who qualify, to hold higher skilled jobs in the Brooklyn plant or elsewhere within the IBM system.
4. Its minimum wages in 1968 were $85 per week, compared with $64 per week which was the legal minimum wage in New York State at that time.

5. It does not use standard IBM tests because they were found to be biased against the disadvantaged.
6. Its criteria for selection are based on two factors: (1) motivation, which was measured by the interviewer's impression of the applicant; and (2) some demonstrated ability for the work, such as passing a test of manual dexterity for assembly jobs.

The initial results of IBM's approach are noteworthy. At the end of the sixth month of operations, the record shows that the plant had met most production quotas and all quality standards.[8] Of the original 290 hired, only 10 percent left the program—3 percent for positive reasons. It was also found that absentee rates were below those usually found in plants primarily hiring the hard-core unemployed.

Admittedly, IBM's success has been the result of unusual dedication and careful planning from management and supporting staff. Such dedication may have been inspired by a "missionary" zeal which is not easily found in typical industrial organizations. Nevertheless, this kind of commitment on the part of the private business sector is the *essential* element needed to complement the worthy social and economic objectives of governmental programs directed at improving the employment opportunities of low-skilled workers.

While emulating the IBM efforts may not be within the capabilities of most industrial establishments, there are some areas in which all employers could be expected to participate in improving the employment opportunities of low-skilled workers. These are mostly related to eliminating various forms of *discrimination.* A few examples of what can be done in this direction are:

1. Less reliance on the Company's own employees as a source of recruitment. Employees usually refer friends and relatives to job openings. This practice generally perpetuates the racial and ethnic composition of the firm's work force.
2. Eliminate unrealistic hiring standards, such as requiring a high school diploma for jobs which traditionally are, or have been, performed by persons with less formal education.
3. Reduce or eliminate use of written tests for hiring or promotion, since they may exclude workers from jobs within their capabilities. In a study[9] of ten blue collar occupations in New York and St. Louis it was found that in eight of the ten occupations, there was no relationship between the workers' educational attainment and their degree of job success.

Elimination of these barriers would greatly enhance the possibilities for employing many unskilled workers, who, in addition to the discrimination barrier, must face other serious problems which affect their employment status.

Low Wages and Welfare Institutions

Employers' discriminatory practices, which exclude blacks and other minorities from reasonably well-paying jobs, have been frequently attacked by some public officials, some minority groups, and some leaders of civic and voluntary agencies, as major reasons for high unemployment among the poor. Newspapers, however, often carry articles about the large numbers of entry-level job openings, and the equally large numbers of unemployed poor.[10] This paradox was explained in part by Daniel P. Moynihan who, in a recent book,[11] said that "as the 1960s wore on the problems of unrealistic expectations began to be compounded by a seeming depreciation of heretofore decent-enough jobs which the poor were now said to find unacceptable."

The director of research for urban social problems at the Center for New York City Affairs, in the New School for Social Research, said in an article[12]

> One of the fascinating statistics about New York City is that fewer persons were employed in domestic service in 1968 than in 1960. This is surely not the result of diminished demand but of a refusal to accept such employment. Yet the rate of pay for domestic workers is $2.00 or more per hour and carfare is extra.
>
> . . . No one who has had the misfortune of staying in a hospital recently, or even visiting one, is untroubled by the shortage of auxiliary and service personnel, a situation which persists despite the long overdue salary increase obtained by the union in recent years. . . [These jobs] do not require a college education, some do not even require a high school graduation, entering skills are often not necessary and racial discrimination is absent or minimal.

Dr. Bernstein sums up the problem by amplifying Moynihan's observation:

> . . . the wholly worthwhile idea of new careers or career ladders has, to some extent, been turned into an ideology which *justifies the refusal of jobs*[a] involving necessary and dignified work if they do not lead ever upward. Somehow an *air of immorality* has been created about the idea of working as a porter or janitor or taxi driver and certainly about urging anyone to do so.

The foregoing statement lead to an examination of the kinds of choices facing the poor in their task to do as well for themselves as they can. Their choices can be seen to consist as a set of decisions to be made within the constraints imposed on them by the labor market *and* by the policies of the welfare administration. If one assumes[13] that most human beings are rational (this includes the poor), or that their behavior can be explained as a rational response to the constraints they face, it may be possible to explain the importance of the welfare system in its role as a deterrent to the employment of the unemployed poor.

For example, there is no incentive for a person to work if the total value in goods and services received from the welfare program exceeds the amount that he could earn by working. In addition, if he takes the value of *leisure* into

[a]Emphasis added.

account, then the person would have to earn more than the welfare benefit to induce him to work.

In New York City, a person with a family of four could receive as much as $73 per week on welfare, with no deductions for tax, social security, or work-related expenses.[14] To match this income, a person's gross salary would have to have been about $95 a week, to cover the costs of transportation, working clothes, and taxes. If, then, for the individual, work has no other value than that received in the form of goods and services purchased with his earnings, then it just does not make any sense for him to take a job unless there is a clear financial reward.

Attention, however, must be focused on the fact that many people stay off welfare even though they are working for the same as, or less than, what is available to them on welfare.[15] In New York City, about 30 percent of the jobs pay between $70 and $90 a week.[16] There are many persons, therefore, who place some intrinsic benefit on working, or who think that even at low wages there is some value attached to not being on welfare. No information is available on the causes which influence some people to work while others decide to go on welfare. In this chapter the hypothesis is introduced that *the decision threshold between working and not working, for low-skilled workers, is largely dependent on the ease of access which they have to job opportunities. The location of a job*, therefore, is regarded as a major determinant of employment. The development of this hypothesis and the calibration of the employment-accessibility model are the subject of the remainder of this chapter.

Transportation Service and Work Trip Mobility in the CBMC Area

The analysis of the transportation variable as the causative effect of unemployment among unskilled workers is based primarily on an empirical study of transportation problems in the Central Brooklyn Model Cities Area of New York City. In the summer of 1969, extensive surveys were made in the CBMC Area to determine, among other things, the unemployment-related problems of poor transit service.

Before developing the mathematical relationship which measures the importance of the quality of transportation access to the employability of the unskilled labor force, it is appropriate to summarize the findings of that study which pertain to work travel. This gives a background of resident labor force characteristics and travel habits.

The CBMC Area is made up of three communities, known as Bedford-Stuyvesant, Brownsville, and a part of East New York. It contains over 404,000 people, 40 percent of whom live in households earning less than $4,000 per year. In 1969, the unemployment rate in the area was 14 percent of the total labor force of 121,000 persons. The predominant population in the area is *black* (78 percent). The other major component of the population is *spanish-speaking* (19 percent), and the remainder is *white*.

Occupational Status of Residents

The occupational status of the CBMC Area population is summarized, by race, in Table 5-4, which separates the labor force into four skill categories, ranging from the *professional-technical* level to the *unskilled laborer*. For all ethnic groups, the unskilled and semiskilled occupations accounted for the largest proportion of the labor force, while the professional/skilled occupations accounted for the smallest proportion.

For the entire CBMC Area, about 70 percent of the people are *not* members of the labor force. The spanish-speaking have the highest representation in this category, and the whites the lowest. This large proportion of nongainful members of the population is largely made up of persons who are young (less than 16 years of age), who account for 60 percent of the nongainful representation.

The age composition of the population identified for each occupational status is shown in Figure 5-1. The young and the elderly are, logically, the groups with the largest representation in the nongainful category.

Unskilled workers represent the largest proportion of labor skills for each age

Table 5-4
Occupational Status of CBMC Residents (breakdown in %)

Occupation[a]	Black	Spanish-Speaking	White	Total
PTMOP	3.6%	2.1%	8.0%	3.3%
SK	3.0	2.6	4.0	3.0
SSK	10.5	7.7	9.3	9.5
USK	14.1	14.9	15.7	13.8
NG	68.8	72.7	63.0	70.4
Total	100.0	100.0	100.0	100.0

[a]Occupation:

PTMOP = Professional, technical and similar classifications; and managers, officials, and similar classifications.

SK = Skilled: craftsmen, foremen, and similar classifications.

SSK = Semiskilled: sales workers, clerical and similar classifications, operatives, and similar workers.

USK = Unskilled: laborers, service workers, private household workers, and occupation not reported.

NG = Nongainful: nonmembers of the labor force.

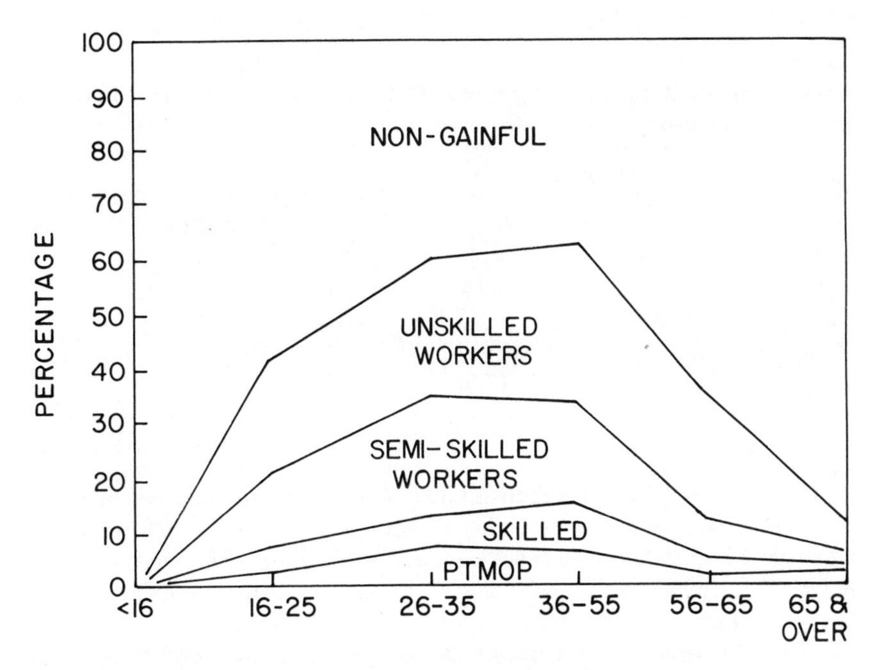

Figure 5-1. Occupation Status of CBMC Population

group. The 36-55 age group has the highest proportion of unskilled workers (30 percent) and, with the exception of the 65-and-over age group, unskilled workers are a significant proportion in every age group. The implications of these findings are relevant to the problem of unemployment, because practically *all* of the unemployment found in the CBMC Area is within the *unskilled labor force.*

Professional/technical and skilled workers, although lowest in proportion when compared to the other labor skills, represent 15.8 percent of the persons in the 36-55 age group, and 12.9 percent of the 26-55 age group. All other age groups are *below* the CBMC population average of 6.3 percent.

As a help in assessing the magnitude of the unemployment problem in the CBMC Area, a general summary of employment characteristics of the labor force is presented in Table 5-5. Although the Area-wide unemployment rate is found to be 14 percent, it can be readily seen that unemployment is *not* equally divided among the four occupational groups, but is instead concentrated primarily in the *unskilled* category. It may also be noted that the largest unemployment concentration is found in the 16-25 age group, with about *one out of two* unskilled persons *not working.*

Car Ownership

The degree of dependence on public transportation for the CBMC Area resident population can be measured by looking at car ownership per household.

Table 5-5
Unemployment Rates by Occupational Status of CBMC Area Labor Force and by Age of Person

Age Group	PTMOP	SK	SSK	USK	Total
16-25	–	–	–	45.0%	22.1%
26-35	0.4%	1.8%	1.1%	29.0	13.2
36-55	–	0.9	1.2	21.6	10.3
56-65	–	–	2.9	37.8	24.2
65 and over	–	–	–	33.3	20.6
Total	0.6	0.9	1.2	29.4	14.0

The members of a household who do *not* own a car will depend completely on public transportation for their travel. Even if, from time to time, occasional trips can be made in a neighbor's or a friend's automobile, non-car-owning household members are basically dependent on a bus, subway, taxicab, or train for a trip which cannot be made on foot.

About 73 percent of the households in the CBMC Area own no car. This compares with 36 percent in the New York Metropolitan Area.[17]

The distribution of non-car-owning households, with respect to income is described in Figure 5-2, which identifies the groups of families with greatest dependence on public transportation for their mobility. The low-income group, which makes up *40 percent* of all households in the Area, contains the largest proportion of households (91 percent) which own no cars.

Modes of Travel to Work

The modes of travel used for work purposes by CBMC Area residents of varying economic states are given in Table 5-6.

While, on the average, over 71 percent of all CBMC workers travel to work in either a subway or a bus, the low-income workers use these two modes more than any other group (78.2 percent vs. 55.4 percent for the high-income worker). The use of an automobile for work purposes is much less likely for the low-income worker than for the high-income worker (12.8 percent vs. 37.8 percent). Most automobile work trips are made by people who drive their own autos, and a very small proportion are passengers, or join a car pool. Car pool use, in fact, is negligible among low-income households.

The use of taxis for work travel is minimal among all income levels. About 7 percent of the low-income workers walked to work. This proportion was lowest for the moderate and middle income categories, but then it appears to rise to about 6 percent for people in the high-income level.

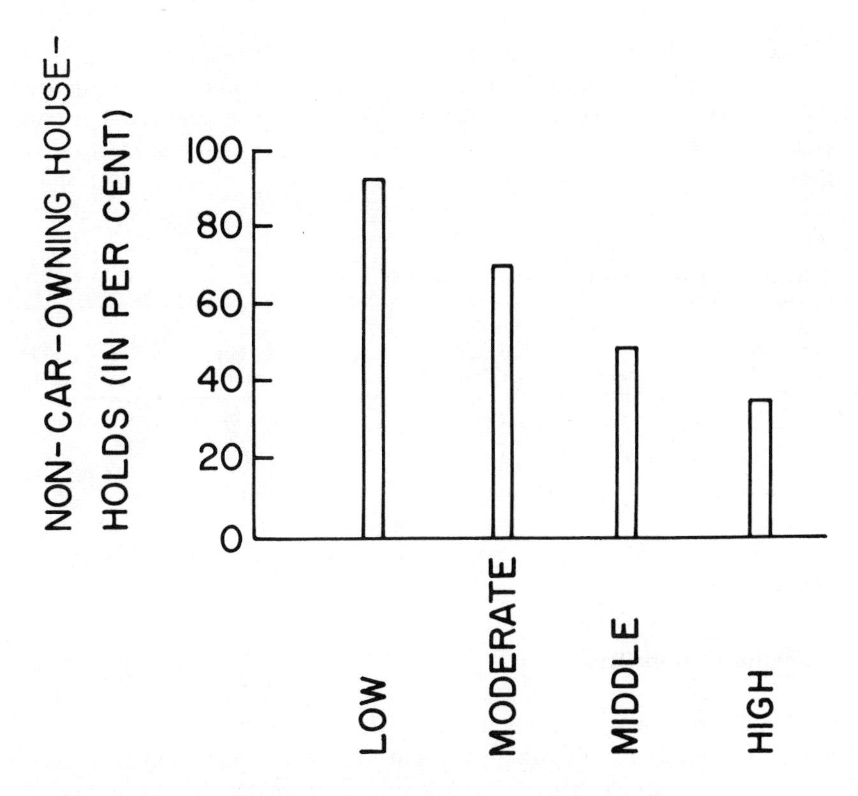

Figure 5-2. Distribution of Non-Car-Owning Households, Related to Income

Table 5-6
Modes of Travel to Work Related to Household Income

	Income Levels[b]				
	Low	Moderate	Middle	High	Total
Auto driver	10.0	18.8	26.2	20.5	18.7
Auto passenger	2.8	3.0	4.1	5.1	3.2
Car pool	–	0.3	1.8	2.3	0.8
Taxi	0.3	1.2	1.1	1.7	1.1
Subway	61.0	50.0	45.4	42.4	51.2
Bus	17.2	22.3	17.6	13.0	20.2
Walking[a]	6.9	3.3	3.0	5.7	3.7
Other	1.8	1.1	0.7	–	0.9

[a]Exceeds 15 minutes.

[b]Low = less than $4,000; Moderate = $4,000-$7,500; Middle = $7,500-$10,000; High = $10,000 and over.

Mode use for work travel was found to be related not only to income levels (and consequently car ownership), but also to the location of a work site (see Table 5-7). Thus, the use of a car to reach work sites in areas well served by mass transit, is considerably less than for those areas where mass transit is not as efficient.

Table 5-7
Job Sites of CBMC Area Workers by Travel Mode

Borough of Employment	Relative Quality of Public Transportation Access to that Borough	Travel by Automobile	Travel by Transit
Brooklyn	Fair-good	65.6%	53.0%
Queens	Very poor	11.4	4.6
The Bronx	Fair-poor	4.1	0.9
Manhattan	Excellent	18.9	41.5
Total		100.0	100.0

Distribution of Work Travel

The CBMC transportation study found that, in New York City, the task of traveling to unskilled job locations is about the same as that required to reach locations which contain skilled jobs. When the jobs are stratified by borough of location and mode of travel access, however, significant differences arise. Using the 85th percentile as the index of comparison, the following observations result: Eighty-five percent of the *professional-technical* jobs located in Brooklyn and Manhattan can be reached in less than 45 minutes by transit. For the remaining three boroughs, the figures are 68 minutes for Queens, 75 minutes for the Bronx, and over one hour and a half for Staten Island. If travel is by automobile, the corresponding figures are 28 minutes for Brooklyn, 39 minutes for Manhattan, 65 minutes for the Bronx, and 85 minutes for Staten Island. Similar observations for the other three skill categories are shown in Table 5-8. In conclusion, the data of Table 5-8 may be summarized as follows:

Table 5-8
Travel Time to Jobs (minutes)

Job Skills	Brooklyn		Manhattan		Queens		The Bronx		Staten Island	
	Transit	Auto	Transit	Auto	Transit	Auto	Transit	Auto	Transit	Auto
Professional-technical	45	28	42	39	68	43	75	65	100	85
Skilled	45	28	42	43	68	43	75	66	100	86
Semiskilled	41	28	42	42	63	42	74	63	100	85
Unskilled	46	29	42	42	67	42	73	64	100	85

1. No travel time differentials exist among the four skill groups.
2. Significant travel time differentials exist to reach jobs located in different boroughs.
3. The boroughs of best transit service are Brooklyn and Manhattan.
4. Jobs in nearby Queens take approximately *50 percent more travel time* by mass transit than those located in either Brooklyn or Manhattan.
5. Jobs located in the Bronx and Staten Island are *highly inaccessible* by mass transit or by automobile.
6. For Manhattan job sites, transit and auto provide *equivalent* travel access.
7. Auto travel time to Brooklyn job sites is approximately *25 percent more efficient* than that provided by mass transit.
8. Auto access to Queens job sites is approximately *one third better* than that provided by mass transit.

Transportation: The Linkage of People and Jobs

The geographic distribution of residences and job locations in an urban area is the result of market forces, which are affected in large measure by the type of transportation system that prevails in the area. Geographic distances, however, can be greatly altered by the transportation network. The spacial distribution of activities in an urban area is therefore perceived according to the level of transportation provided. This implies that the amount of travel occurring between different activity sites is largely a function of the travel time required to reach a potential destination.

Transportation studies have shown that people tend to economize, and try to keep from traveling farther than necessary.[18]

The way in which people react to travel opportunities is an important characteristic, and one which must be taken into account in planning for transportation facilities designed to improve access to urban activities. For this reason, therefore, it is essential that plans be developed to conform with the travel habits of the population which is to benefit from transportation improvements.

The population group of interest in this analysis is the low-income unskilled worker. And the question which must be answered is: how far away can a job site be from his residence before it ceases to be attractive? What we are looking for is the effect of travel time on work travel.

Assuming that the wage rates are not significantly different from location to location,[b] that a near-uniform distribution of unskilled job types exists in every area of employment, and that a worker is likely to accept employment without regard to preferential location within the city, we could attribute the observed intensity of work travel to two factors: transportation access, and the number of employment opportunities located within an area.

[b]This condition was observed in the CBMC Area.

A well-known and widely used method of trip distribution in the transportation planning literature is the "Gravity Model."[19] This model is based on the concept that travel is a function of the forces which attract trips to a given area, and the travel time required to get there. Applied to work trips, for example, the model states that the employment potential of an employment center is directly related to its size and inversely related to its proximity to the labor force. In other words, the larger the center and the closer it is to the labor force, the more workers will go there for employment.

Expressed in mathematical form, the *gravity model* is shown below in its simplest form:

$$WT_{i\text{-}j} = WT_i \frac{E_j / d_{i\text{-}j}^{(\alpha)}}{\sum_{j=1}^{n} E_j / d_{i\text{-}j}^{(\alpha)}} \tag{5.1}$$

where

WT_{i-j} = Volume of work trips of the employed labor force residing in zone (i) and going to zone (j)

WT_i = Total number of workers who reside in zone (i)

E_j = Size of employment in zone (j)

d_{i-j} = Distance (usually expressed in travel time) between residential zone (i) and employment zone (j)

α = An exponent applied to the distance variable.

The above model states that an employment center (E_j) in zone (j) attracts workers:

1. in *direct* proportion to the number of employees in zone (i), i.e., WT_i;
2. in *direct* proportion to its size, E_j;
3. in *inverse* proportion to the distance from the worker's residence ($d_{i\text{-}j}^{(\alpha)}$); and
4. in *inverse* proportion to competing employment centers:

$$\sum_{j=1}^{n} \frac{E_j}{d_{i\text{-}j}^{\alpha}} \tag{5.2}$$

Using the gravity model to reproduce the distribution of travel in an area requires several trial runs with assumed values of α, the exponent of the distance variable. Once calibration is achieved, the expression $1/(d_{i\text{-}j})^{\alpha}$ in the model may be interpreted as *the numerical representation of the effect of travel time on trip making.* This spacial parameter, called the *travel time factor,* $F_{i\text{-}j}$, was obtained for the unskilled work trip distribution in the CBMC Area, and is shown in Figure 5-3. $F_{i\text{-}j}$ may be thought of as a variable which inhibits the propensity of travel for unskilled workers. For example, employment zones which are located far away are much less effective in attracting unskilled CBMC Area workers than are employment zones which are located close to their residences. From Figure 5-3, it may be seen that jobs which are 15 minutes away are *8 times* more effective than jobs located one hour away from the unskilled worker's residence; and as the travel distance required to reach a job site reaches an hour and a half, the effectiveness of such a job site as a source of employment for a CBMC Area unskilled worker is virtually negligible.

Although the cost of commuting to work may also affect the work trip distribution, the importance of the cost variable was not relevant in the model because most of the work trips take place within the one-fare zone which covers a large part of New York City's job supply. In some cases, however, the transit routing for commuting to job sites is extremely complex, and involves transferring at several points, and if more than one fare is used, the travel time could be

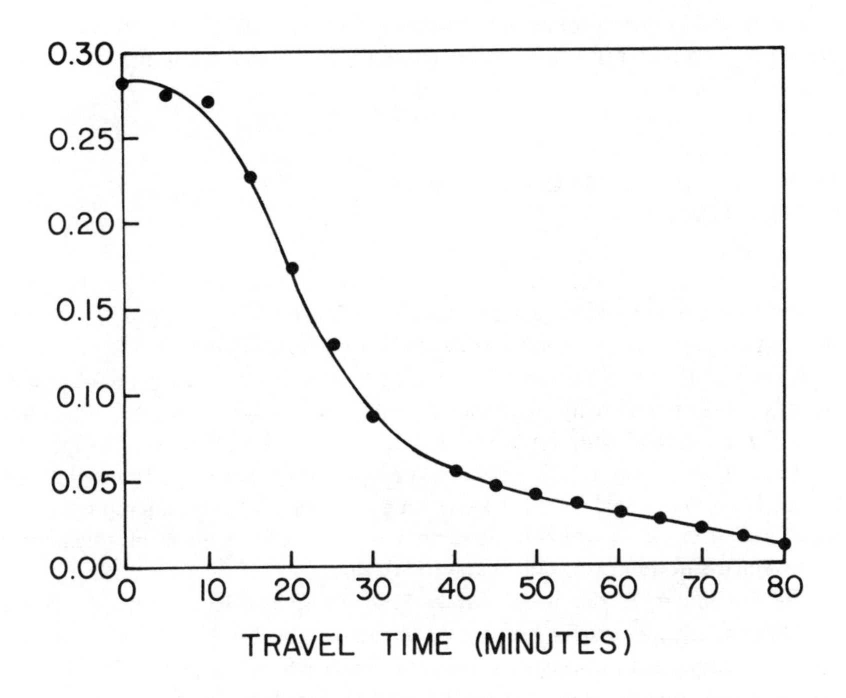

Figure 5-3. Travel Time Factor for Unskilled Work Trips

effectively reduced by about 10 minutes per transfer. In these few cases, transit access times to industrial areas were calculated on the basis of one-fare travel time, thus reflecting the additional cost barrier if more than one fare was paid to reduce travel time. Since, on the average, the payment of an extra fare involved the saving of about 10 minutes, using the one-fare travel time in the model implies equating the cost of one transit fare to 10 minutes of travel time, or valuing the unskilled worker's travel time at $1.20 per hour.

Employment and Transportation Access: A Quantitative Model

The typical low-income or unskilled worker in the CBMC Area is entirely dependent on mass transportation for his travel to work. The very few (less than 1 out of 10) who can use a car as an alternative mode of travel have exhibited a greater choice of work opportunities and are therefore at a significant advantage in finding and holding a job. But even for these few the car is seldom a dependable travel mode, since the cars owned by the poor are typically older and in need of frequent repairs.[20]

The accessibility-employment hypothesis developed in this section states that the unemployment rate in a residential area is a function of the quality of transportation service from that area to suitable job sites.

Assumptions Made for Model Development: Cause and Effect

An individual either works or does not. For an unskilled member of the labor force whose annual income seldom exceeds $4,000 before taxes, the probability of his employment is assumed to be dependent on several factors.

There will be some people who, due to their individual characteristics, will (1) only work occasionally at so-called "odd jobs" or seasonal jobs, or (2) become "discouraged" with seriously looking for work. These people manage somehow to live, from public assistance or by earning their living through illegal means. This group could be classified as long-term, or hard-core, unemployed. As such, therefore, it is *unlikely* that they will benefit from even substantial improvements in transportation access to job sites.

The remainder of the unskilled workers' group consists of people whose employment characteristics are largely dependent on the job market and the forces of public institutions (primarily welfare), which compete with the job market in influencing the employability of an unskilled worker.[21]

It is not intended, however, to discuss the sociological and psychological factors which affect the individual preferences that influence an unskilled person in the choice of working or not working. Instead, just as it is standard practice in economic analysis to take tastes and attitudes as given, the approach taken in the development of the employment-transportation model assumes that all unskilled workers, whether they work or do not work, exhibit an aggregate behavior which is essentially identical when they rationalize the choice between working and not working.

The concept implicit in the employment-accessibility model is that the quality of public transportation service from a worker's residence to a potential job site will affect his choice of working or not working, *et ceteris paribus.* Thus the unskilled unemployment rate in a residential area is expected to vary according to some measure of transportation quality which expresses the *ease of access* from that area to job sites suitable to the unskilled worker.

Cause and Effect

In the study of urban problems such as economics, transportation, employment, and a whole host of social issues, one is primarily concerned with cause-and-effect relationships. This concern stems from the need for establishing policies and courses of action to bring about effective solutions to serious problems.

The employment-accessibility model which is presented in this chapter is one such attempt in establishing and measuring a cause-and-effect relationship between transportation accessibility and employment.

In general, to *prove* that one variable causes an effect on another variable is not an easy task. In most cases, in fact, there is no failure-free proof. Logic and common sense are the best means to use in avoiding variables which are not fundamentally related.

The simplest concept of causation is one according to which one particular event (the "cause") is followed by another particular event (the "effect"). For example, if a proper switch is flipped the electric light goes on, and if it is flipped back again, the light goes off.

In justifying the effect of transportation accessibility on unemployment, however, a more complex logic is required.

An earlier section of this chapter related unemployment to several nontransportation variables. Since the nontransportation variables are assumed to affect low-skilled workers equally, regardless of where they lived in the CBMC Area, it is possible to isolate the transportation variable as the only variable which varies from subarea to subarea. Caution, however, should be exercised with this approach. This refers to the possibility that the association between transportation accessibility and employment levels might, in fact, be due to the phenomenon that the unemployed *might* live in low rent areas, and low rent areas *might* be found where there is poor transportation accessibility. Thus, if this were the case, there would be no cause and effect between transportation and employment levels. Unfortunately, no rent data are available for the CBMC Area to compare rents paid by welfare and low-income households as a function of their transportation accessibility to work places. There is strong evidence, however, that rent differentials, if any, might not be present:

1. In New York City the Welfare Department reimburses the clients for the cost of rents thus eliminating the incentive to shop for "low cost" housing.
2. The Long Island Study[22] found that the average monthly rents for poverty and welfare households were *higher* than the average rent paid in the seven communities surveyed: $173 vs. $165 per month in Suffolk County and $110 vs. $104 per month in Nassau County.

It seems safe, then, to eliminate the possibility of the rent differential concept as the underlying cause for unemployment variations among the low-skilled workers in the CBMC Area.

We should recall at this point that most of the unemployment in the CBMC Area is attributable to the unskilled workers. Other labor force members exhibited extremely low unemployment rates (see Table 5-5). Labor force members who are *not* unskilled, however, also live within the same areas occupied by the unskilled worker. Why is it, then, that they exhibit low unemployment and are seemingly not affected by poor transportation? The answer to this question will illustrate the rationale for using transportation accessibility as the logical causative variable which tends to inhibit employment of low skilled workers.

The earnings of skilled workers are considerably higher than those of unskilled workers. The skilled worker, therefore, has no substitute source of income which would permit him to provide for his family at the same level that he can while working. He is willing then, to keep his job even if he must make a complicated and time-consuming trip. His probability of working, therefore, is always very high, even when transportation access to his job is very poor (see Figure 5-4).

For the unskilled worker, however, whose annual wages are low, the incentive to work is low, because the income that he can earn by working can also be provided by public assistance. In the present social system, therefore, the transportation element may be viewed as the causative variable which affects the employment status of the low-income worker. It is postulated, then, that the probability of employment for unskilled workers varies as a function of their accessibility to work places. This is illustrated in Figure 5-5.

It should be added, however, that if the choice were between working and starvation, the low-income worker, just as the higher income worker, would not be sensitive to the transportation variable, and no cause-and-effect relationship could be justified in the employment-accessibility model.

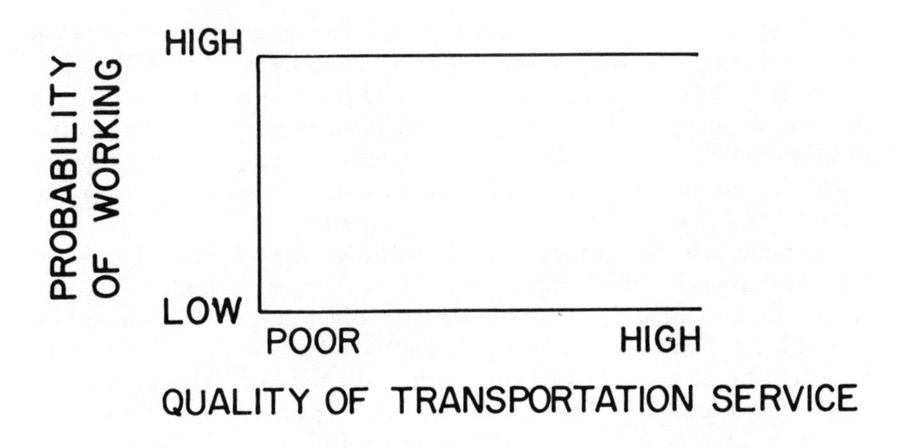

Figure 5-4. The Decision to Work for Skilled Workers

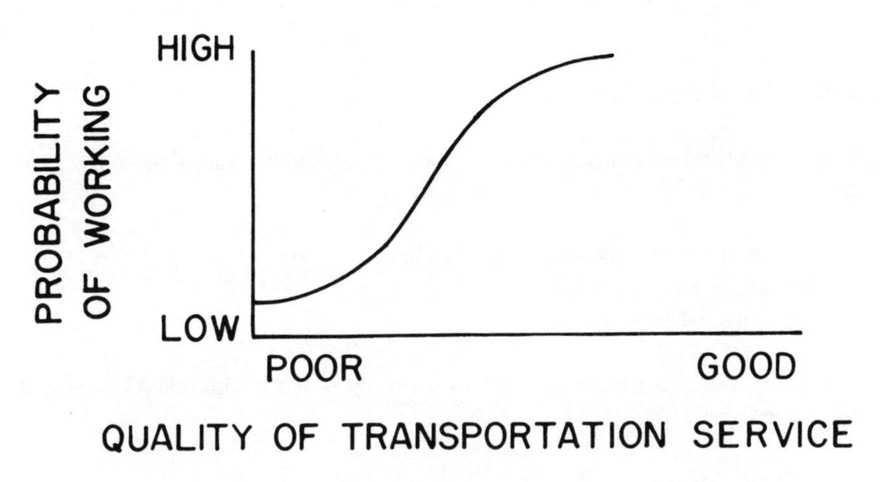

Figure 5-5. The Decision to Work for Unskilled Workers

Description of Data Base

Because most of the poor have no automobiles, and the cost of a taxi for commuting purposes is unreasonably high, the transportation facilities considered as providing access to jobs are only the bus and subway modes. In addition, because the data on job openings is not available, the total employment figures estimated for an area are used as a proxy for the potential for employment in that area. It is assumed that on the average, the number of job openings in an employment zone are proportional to the number of filled jobs. Although this assumption does not provide a sufficient basis for recommending the type of transportation services required for improving access to job sites which are poorly served by mass transportation, it is felt that for the purpose of calibrating the proposed hypothesis, this simplification of the problem still provides the data necessary for calibrating the model.

Since the bulk of unemployment in the CBMC Area consists of unskilled labor force members, the transportation access analysis is confined to those jobs suitable for the unskilled, and for which data is readily available. Only those jobs located within New York City are considered for model calibration. This was the result of the observed travel characteristics of employed unskilled workers, whose work trips, for all practical purposes, were exclusively made within New York City. The results of the model are in no way constrained by this latter restriction, because if all job sites are included, regardless of their location within the metropolitan area, the required travel time and cost to reach these jobs (with the present transit system) would be considered *excessive* by the unskilled worker, who rarely makes a trip which takes longer than one hour.[23]

Calculation of Travel Time

Transit travel times from residences to jobs are calculated from peak-hour transit operation. Added to station-to-station riding time are:

1. Time required to walk to a subway, or bus.
2. Time spent waiting for the vehicle.
3. Time required to walk to the job site.

Peak-hour transit operations are used because most work trips take place within this period.

Accessibility Measures

Accessibility may be described as the ease of travel from one area to other areas.

Since trips are made to satisfy a particular desire, accessibility measures are usually related to the set of activities which may satisfy the purpose of the particular trip. Thus, to measure accessibility to jobs requires knowledge of (1) where the activities (E_j) are located and (2) the parameter of separation ($T_{i\text{-}j}$) between a residential area (R_i) and the places of employment (E_j).

Hence, it may be hypothesized that residential accessibility to job sites is a function of the number of jobs and the travel time required to reach these jobs, or:

$$X_i = f(E_{jk}, T_{i\text{-}j}) \tag{5.3}$$

where

X_i = Accessibility to jobs of zone i

E_{jk} = Number of jobs of type (k) located in zone (j)

$T_{i\text{-}j}$ = Travel time required to travel between zones (i) and (j).

If travel time is held constant, say at 30 or 45 minutes, the accessibility to the jobs of a zone becomes a measure of the number of jobs that could be reached within this travel time interval, or

$$X_i = \Sigma E_j / T_{i\text{-}j} \leqslant 30 \text{ min.} \tag{5.4}$$

Another measure of accessibility might be the weighted travel time required to reach all jobs within the area, or

$$X_i = \frac{\Sigma E_j T_{i\text{-}j}}{\Sigma E_j} \tag{5.5}$$

Equations (5.4) and (5.5) are easy to understand but do not provide for a complete and accurate determination of accessibility. For example, Equation (5.4) includes only those jobs within a specified travel time (30 minutes), and takes no account of the potential effect of jobs located beyond this boundary. The travel time boundary could be expanded to include all jobs, but this approach would result in values of X_i's which would be identical for each zone.

Equation (5.5) is weak because it does not consider that travel time is perceived as a nonlinear variable by the traveler, and it assumes that jobs are normally distributed about the mean. Where this latter assumption is not found [see Figure 5-6(b)], the mean values of travel time calculated from Equation

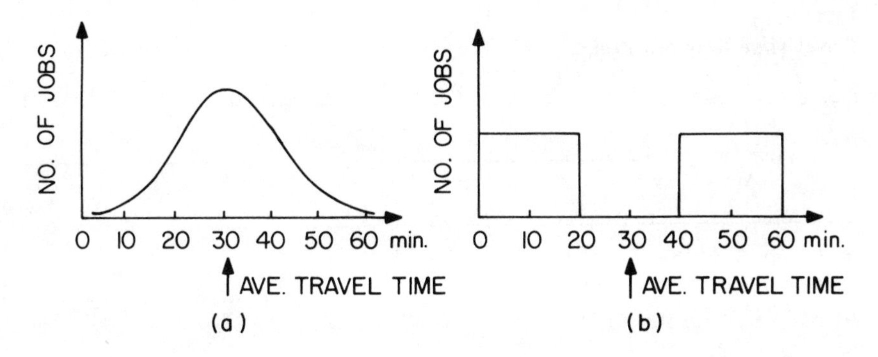

Figure 5-6. Distribution of Jobs vs. Travel Time (TT) From Zone of Residence

(5.5) for each zone are not comparable. For example, under the normal distribution the mean travel time for Zone 1 adequately represents the central tendency of job concentration around the mean value. But in the case of the uniform bimodal distribution for Zone 2, the mean value is a poor descriptor of job dispersion. Therefore, although the two zones may have identical average travel time values, their accessibilities to jobs are definitely not the same.

A more appropriate measure of accessibility is found in the following expression:

$$X_i = \sum_{j=1}^{n} \frac{E_j}{(T_{ij})^{\alpha}} \quad (5.6)$$

It may be seen that Equation (5.6) corresponds to the denominator of the Gravity Model of trip distribution discussed earlier. The numerical value of this equation represents an index of accessibility. Thus, for an area containing (n) residential zones, (n) accessibility indices would be obtained, and those zones with the higher numerical values have the higher accessibilities. Conceptually, Equation (5.6) is appealing, because it states that accessibility increases with an increase in the number of jobs, or with a decrease in travel time. In addition, it states that the effect of travel time is perceived as a *disutility*, which varies with the power (α) of travel time.

The exponent (α) of travel time was calibrated by observing the distribution of work travel for unskilled CBMC Area workers. This was discussed earlier, where the travel time factor, $1/(T_{ij})^{\alpha}$, or F_{ij}, was illustrated in Figure 5-3.

An example will illustrate the use of Equation (5.6). Let there be an area containing four industrial areas E_1, E_2, E_3, E_4 and three residential zones R_1, R_2, R_3, as shown in Figure 5-7.

The required transit travel times from residential areas to industrial areas are shown in Table 5-9.

Table 5-9
Travel Time Between Zones

Residential Areas	Industrial Areas			
	E_1	E_2	E_3	E_4
R_1	10	20	25	30
R_2	20	40	45	60
R_3	25	50	55	40

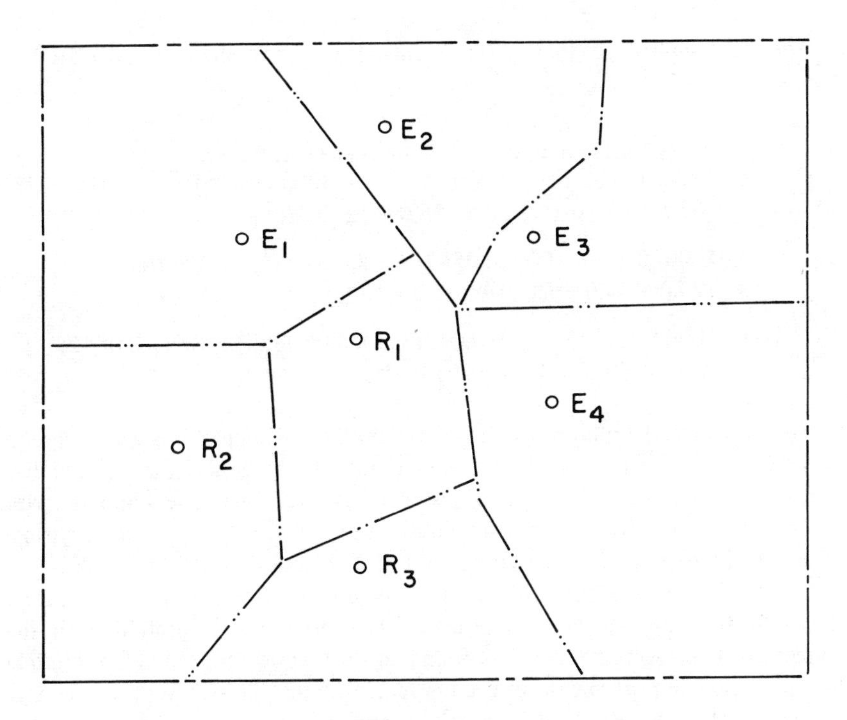

Figure 5-7. Hypothetical Study Area

The number of unskilled jobs located in each industrial area is

$$E_1 = 1000 \text{ jobs}$$
$$E_2 = 1000 \text{ jobs}$$
$$E_3 = 3000 \text{ jobs}$$
$$E_4 = 5000 \text{ jobs}$$

From Figure 5-4 the travel time factors ($F_{i\text{-}j}$) associated with each trip length are:

Travel Time ($T_{i\text{-}j}$)	Travel Time Factor ($F_{i\text{-}j}$)
10 minutes	0.2575
20 minutes	0.1700
25 minutes	0.1200
30 minutes	0.0856
40 minutes	0.0542
45 minutes	0.0450
50 minutes	0.0400
55 minutes	0.0357
60 minutes	0.0286

The accessibility to jobs of each zone (X_i) may then be calculated as follows:

$$X_1 = (E_1)(F_{1\text{-}1}) + E_2(F_{1\text{-}2}) + E_3(F_{1\text{-}3}) + E_4(F_{1\text{-}4})$$
$$= 1000\,(0.257\text{x}5) + 1000\,(0.0170) + 3000\,(0.125) + 5000\,(0.085\text{x}6)$$
$$= 257.5 + 170.0 + 375.0 + 428.0 = 1230.5$$

$$X_2 = 1000\,(0.17) + 1000\,(0.0542) + 3000\,(0.045) + 5000\,(0.0286)$$
$$= 170.0 + 54.0 + 135.0 + 143.0 = 502.0$$

$$X_3 = 1000\,(0.120) + 1000\,(0.040) + 3000\,(0.0357) + 5000\,(0.0542)$$
$$= 120.0 + 40.0 + 107.1 + 271.0 = 538.1$$

The accessibility indices resulting from the above calculations can be useful only when they are compared with one another. It can be said that accessibility measures are *relative* values which describe how well one zone compares with another. In the example we can see that Zone 1 is more than twice as accessible to jobs as Zones 2 or 3, while the accessibilities of Zones 2 and 3 are similar.

The analytical strength of this accessibility variable, however, goes far beyond the need for ranking zones in terms of this measure. Its usefulness in the employment-accessibility model is found in its unique property of *translating* transportation improvements into employment gains. This is done by relating unemployment levels (UR_i) to accessibility indices (X_i):

$$UR_i = f(X_i) \qquad (5.7)$$

Since $X_i = f(E_j$ and $T_{ij})$, an improvement in either E_j or T_{ij} can be directly translated into its corresponding effect on the unemployment reduction for the zone affected.

The functional relationship of unemployment and accessibility is now established for the CBMC Area using the data from that study.

Model Calibration

The impact of transportation accessibility on unemployment levels of the unskilled labor force is obtained by relating the two variables through *regression analysis.*

The CBMC Area was divided into seventy-eight analysis zones. An average zone was 41.8 acres, and contained approximately 5,200 persons. Accessibility indices were calculated for each zone in the same manner as in the above illustrative example. Zones of equal accessibility were combined; twelve analysis areas resulted. In each of these analysis areas, the unskilled labor force was divided into two groups: those who worked and those who were unemployed.

The unemployment rate for each analysis area, together with the accessibility index of the area, are shown in Table 5-10.

The unemployment rates indicated in Table 5-10 contain all unskilled workers who are unemployed. No data was obtained from the CBMC Area transportation study which would separate the hard-core, or chronically, unemployed from the rest. A hand-fitted line to this data, shown in Figure 5-8,

Table 5-10
Accessibility Index and Unemployment of Unskilled Workers, by CBMC Analysis Area

Analysis Area Identification	CBMC Identification[a]	Accessibility Index (in 100,000)	Unemployment Rate (in %)
1	BR & ENY	1.8	33.0
2	BR & ENY	2.0	28.5
3	BR & ENY	2.2	28.5
4	BR & ENY	2.4	28.0
5	BR & ENY	2.6	26.5
6	BR & ENY	2.8	23.0
7	BS	3.0	35.0
8	BS	3.2	22.0
9	BS	3.4	34.5
10	BS	3.6	23.5
11	BS	4.0	27.5
12	BS	4.2	19.5

[a]BR = Brownsville; ENY = East New York; BS = Bedford-Stuyvesant.

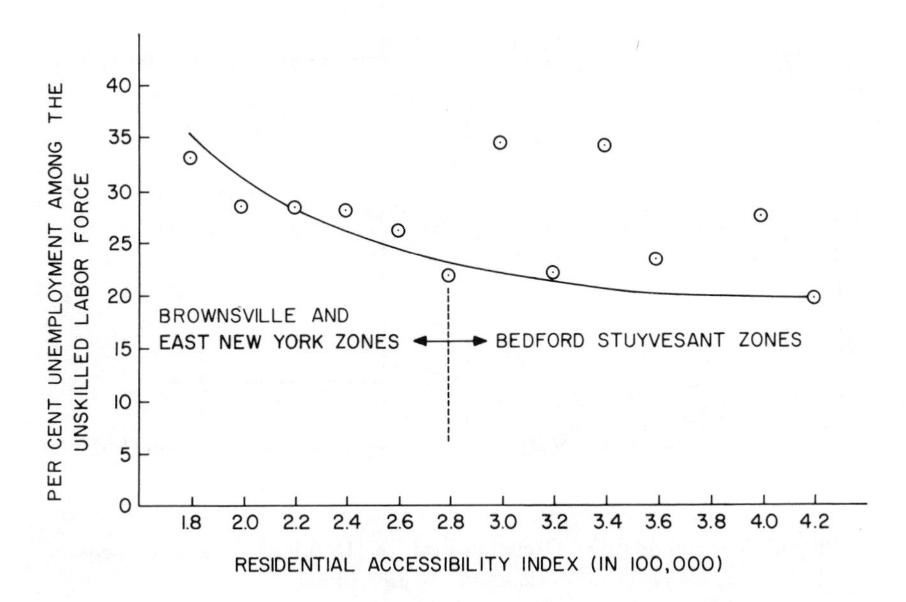

Figure 5-8. The Unemployment-Accessibility Relationship

indicates that the correlation sought between unemployment and accessibility is not clearly confirmed by the data. In fact, even if a high correlation *were* visible, this does not immediately lead to the conclusion that there is cause and effect.

As was previously observed, it is important to divide unemployment data into two categories: one set includes those who are hard-core or chronically unemployed, the other comprises unemployed persons who *may respond* to transportation improvements. This concept is illustrated (in its extreme cases) in Figure 5-9, where we see that there is apparently no relationship between unemployment and transportation accessibility (a) when the hard-core unemployed are not separated from the rest. When this is done, however, the relationship (which in (a) is "clouded" by the presence of the hard-core unemployed) is clearly visible in (b).

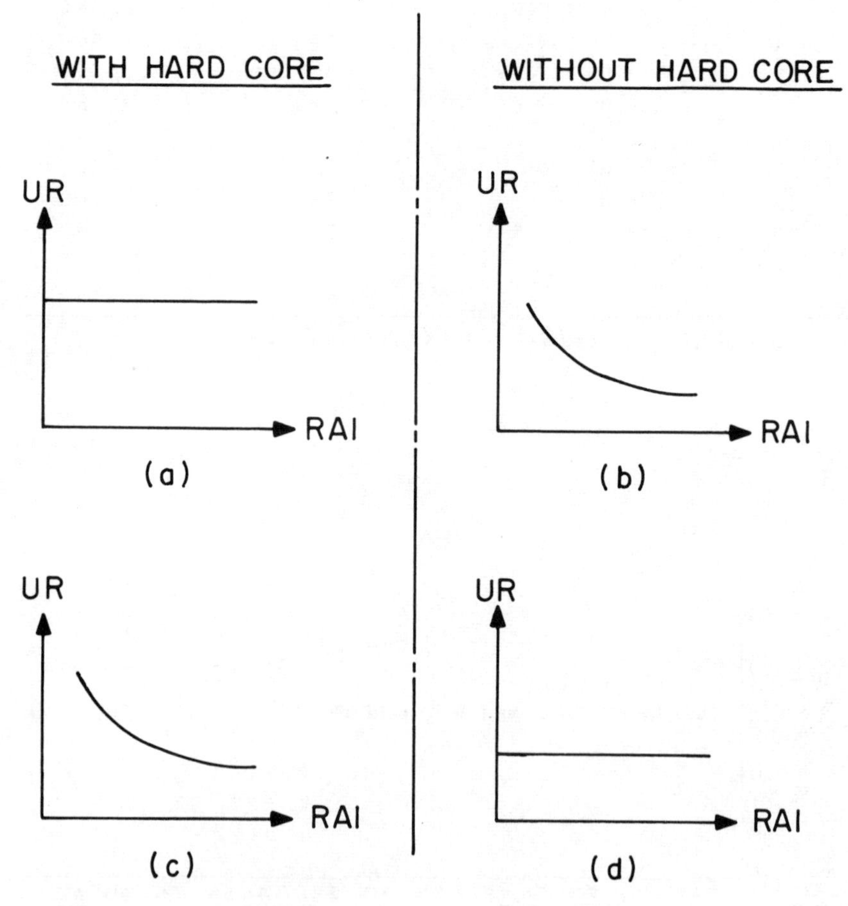

Figure 5-9. Hypothetical Relationships of Unskilled Unemployment Rate vs. Transportation Accessibility to Job Sites

Similarly, (c) illustrates that it is possible to measure a causal effect of transportation on unemployment when the hard-core are *not* separated from total unemployment. This occurrence, however, may be the result of the propensity of the hard-core unemployed to reside primarily in zones of poor accessibility to job sites. When the hard-core unemployed are removed, therefore, there may be little or no correlation between the unemployment and accessibility variables, as shown in (d).

For these reasons, the unemployment rate variable calculated for the CBMC Area was made to conform with the requirement that it should not contain hard-core or chronically unemployed individuals. These adjustments were possible at the community level from a study[23] made available by the Central Brooklyn Model Cities Office. It was thus determined that, in Bedford-Stuyvesant, about 61 percent of the unskilled unemployment represented hard-core unemployment. For Brownsville and East New York, the corresponding figure was 39 percent. Based on these estimates, the unemployment rates calculated for the CBMC Area transportation study were separated into hard-core and non-hard-core unemployment, as shown in Table 5-11.

The results obtained in using non-hard-core unemployment *only* are illustrated in Figure 5-9. It may be noted, by a cursory comparison of Figures 5-8 and 5-10, that this latter scatter diagram displays a more definitive pattern of association between the unemployment and accessibility variables. It appears,

Table 5-11
Accessibility Index, Hard Core, and Non-Hard-Core Unemployment, by CBMC Analysis Area

Analysis Area Identification	CBMC Identification[a]	Accessibility Index (in 100,000)	Hard-Core Unemployment (%)	Non-Hard-Core Unemployment (%)
1	BR & ENY	1.8	12.9%	20.1%
2	BR & ENY	2.0	11.1	17.4
3	BR & ENY	2.2	11.1	17.4
4	BR & ENY	2.4	10.9	17.1
5	BR & ENY	2.6	10.4	16.1
6	BR & ENY	2.8	9.0	14.0
7	BS	3.0	21.4	13.6
8	BS	3.2	13.4	8.6
9	BS	3.4	21.0	13.5
10	BS	3.6	14.4	9.1
11	BS	4.0	16.8	10.7
12	BS	4.2	11.9	7.6

[a]BR = Brownsville; ENY = East New York; BS = Bedford-Stuyvesant.

further, that the relationship might be described by a *negative exponential function*, of the type:

$$UR = a + e^{-k(RAI)} \tag{5.8}$$

The negative exponential function is conceptually appealing, because it states that the importance of the accessibility variable on unemployment *decreases* as accessibility *increases.* For example, according to the hand-fitted line, a greater reduction in unemployment is obtained from a 20,000-unit increase in accessibility if the initial accessibility of an area was measured at 200,000 instead of 360,000 units.

For ease of computation, the *negative exponential function* may be transformed to a *linear function*, using a logarithmic transformation, and then fitting the linear function to the data by linear regression, using the *least-square method.* In this way the final employment-accessibility model takes the following form:

$$Y = a + b \log_{10} X \tag{5.9}$$

where

Y = the Unemployment rate in percent

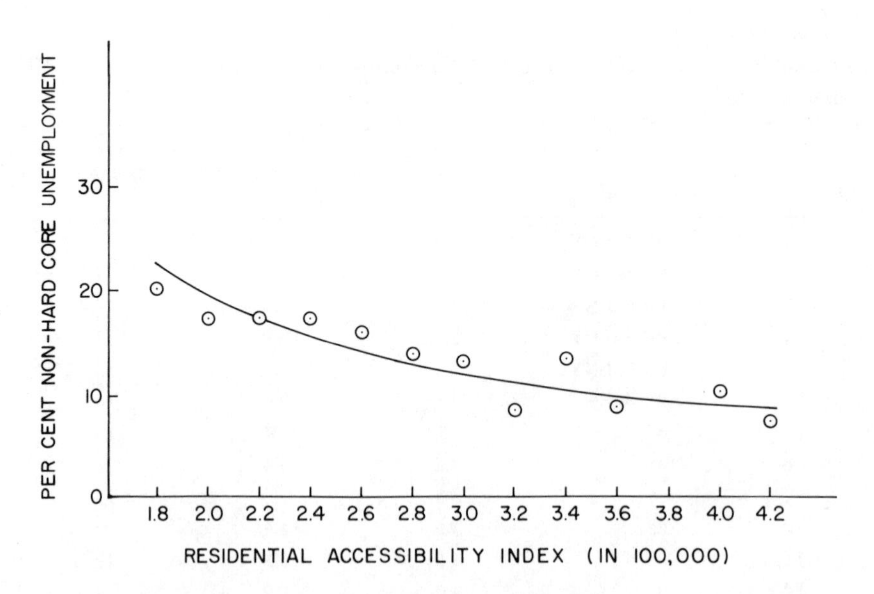

Figure 5-10. Non-Hard-Core Unskilled Unemployment vs. Residential Accessibility

and

X = the Residential Accessibility Index.

The calibrated form of the model (see also Figure 5-11) in the CBMC Area is:

$$Y = 186.26 - 31.65 \log_{10} X \qquad (5.10)$$

The correlation coefficient (r) was 0.93, and the standard error of estimate $S_{y.x}$ = 1.61 percent. It may therefore be concluded that the transportation accessibility variable *significantly affects the unemployment levels* of the unskilled labor force living in the CBMC Area.

The Utility of the Model

The results of the employment-accessibility analysis may be summarized as follows:

1. The employment-accessibility hypothesis was found valid for the CBMC Area.
2. About 11.5 percent of the non-hard-core unskilled unemployment in the CBMC Area is attributable to lack of adequate transportation to job sites.

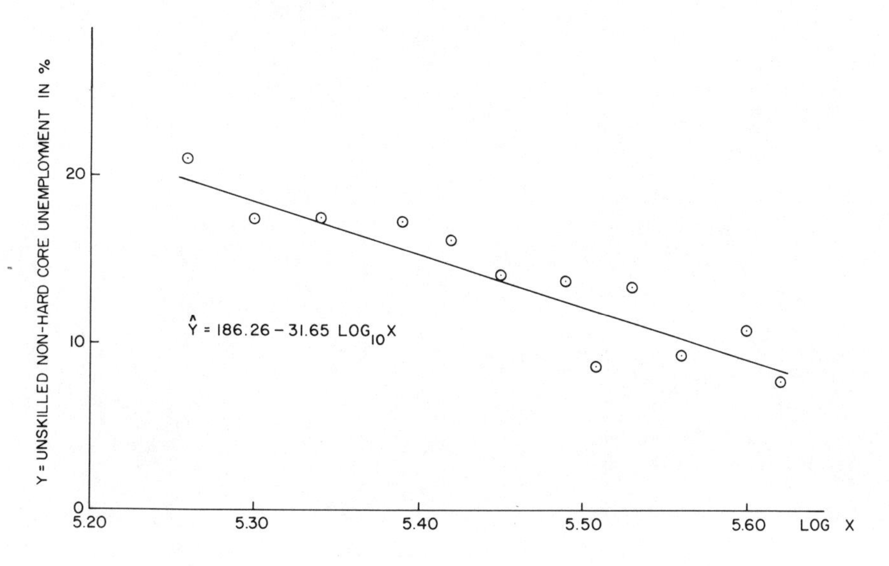

Figure 5-11. The Employment-Accessibility Model

3. The unemployment reduction that can be expected in an area depends on the increase in accessibility programmed for the area and the level of existing transportation service found in the area.
4. Since the model parameters were found through calibration, the model is, of necessity, *site-specific*, and cannot be used in other areas in its present structure. The model should undergo calibration if intended for use in other areas, to reflect the prevailing conditions.
5. The model is intended for use in short-range planning projects.
6. The model's most desirable feature is that it permits more comprehensive cost-benefit analyses of transportation improvements to job sites. This occurs because the model estimates the social benefits accruing as a result of increased employment. These benefits consist primarily of reducing the costs which society must bear to subsidize the income of the unemployed.

In a following chapter, examples are developed for the purpose of illustrating the use of the model primarily as it regards item 6. above.

6 Improving Mobility for the Young, the Aged, and the Handicapped

The Psychology of "Life Space"

"Life space" as noted by Gelwicks[1] represents an abstraction of a physical/sociological/psychological description of human activity. The term apparently began with Lewin[2] as descriptive of an inner psychology; Bach and Gergen[3] spoke of "effective life space" as the area of the world which a person would accept as related to his own conduct. Smith[4] spoke of it in terms of capacity, contacts, and self-image. Gelwicks[5] redefines it into "zones," including *man, personal space, home range, physical world,* and *psychological world.* Of these aspects of life space we are concerned with the "home range," defined by Gelwicks as:

> An ameboid signature whose pattern is formed by a series of behavior settings, oriented towards a predominant locus of activity (usually the place of residence), and connected by significant linkages and settings traversed and occupied by the individual in his normal activities. Occasional trips outside this series are not considered part of the home range. In addition, merely connecting the outlying points of the home range gives a false impression of the actual area covered and may indicate a larger range than really exists. Physical mobility and transportation play a major role in determining the boundaries of the home range. Transportation is in effect a channel penetrating all zones of the life space.[6]

This concept can be illustrated in Figure 6-1a,b,c.

In 6-1a, the "ameboid signature" is formed by extending a transportation corridor out from "home" to each common "behavior setting." In 6-1b, we "merely connect the outlying points of the home range," providing the "false impression of the actual area covered." In 6-1c, we can present a more idealized version of the same life space (and even more false an impression) by using the furthest "behavior setting," the school, as the radius of an area theoretically covered by the child's "home range."

Using, then, the "ameboid signature" as the most logical representation, we can show the relative expansion of life space with growth and maturity and its consequent contraction with age (Figure 6-2a,b,c, and d).

The circular life space representation is shown in Figure 6-3a,b,c, and d.

At any rate, the life space expands with maturity and contracts with age. As Gelwicks puts it: "the principal character of [the older person's] life space may

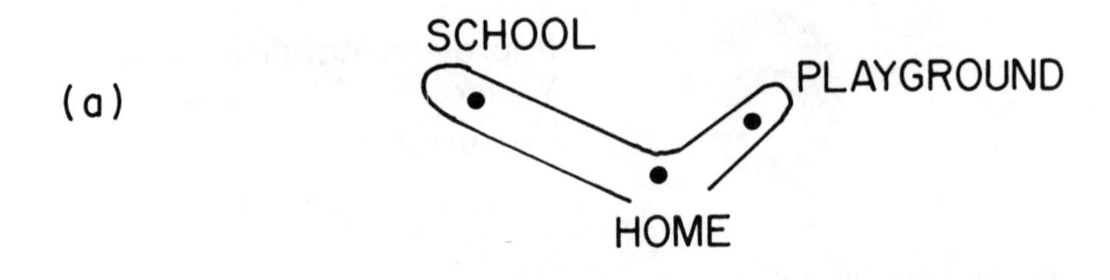

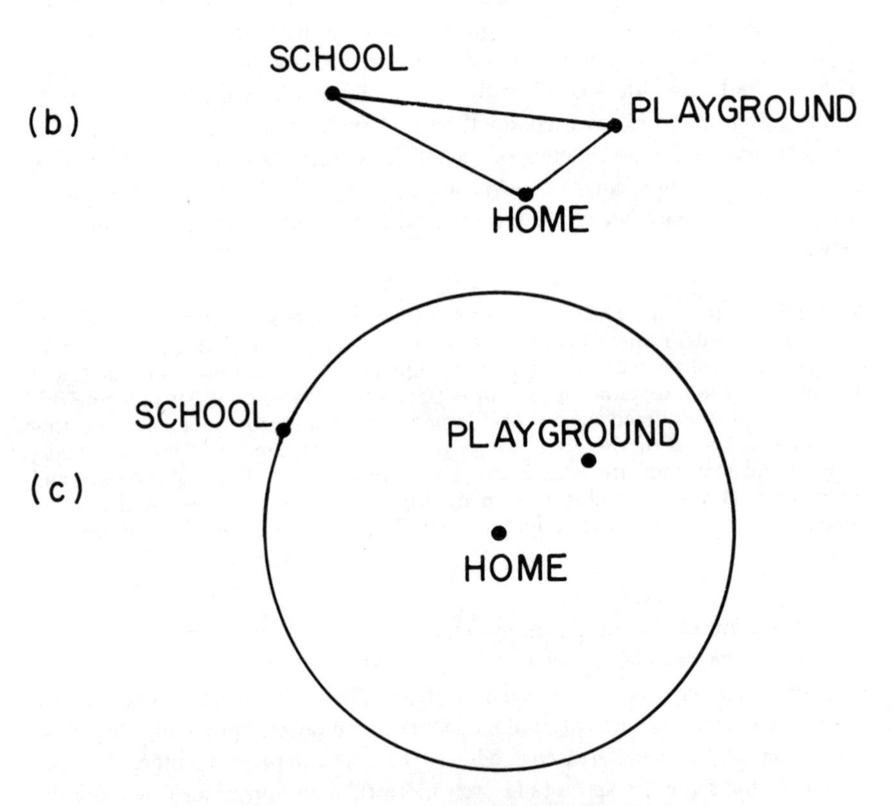

Figure 6-1. Life Space of Small Child

be described as follows: the quality and size diminishes; static relationships replace dynamic ones; there is less differentiation within the life space, particularly within the home range; boundaries become less flexible and less permeable; and the number and quality of channels are reduced."

What, then, is the basis of "life space," its extension and diminution with

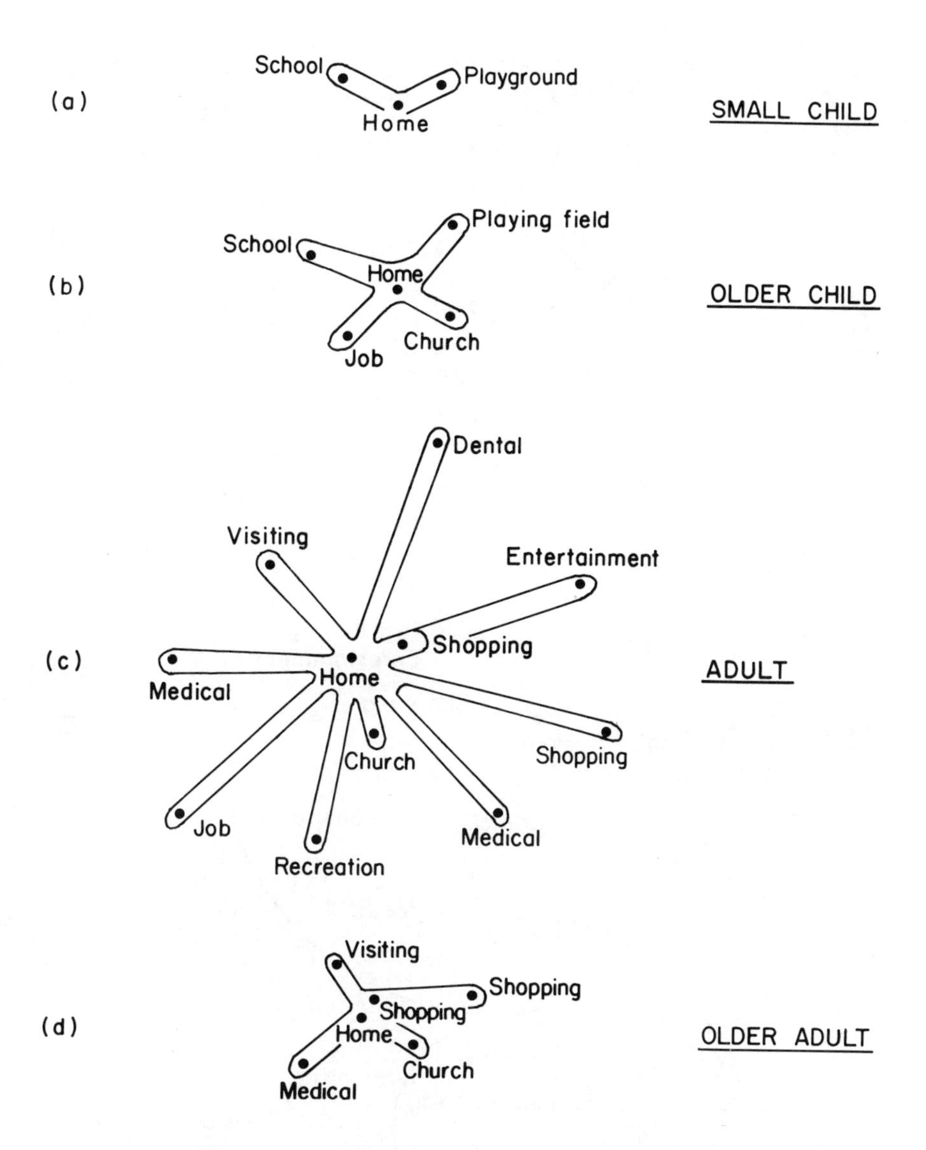

Figure 6-2. Life Space of Ages of Man (Amoebic)

time? It is physical, it is economic, and it is psychological. The young child goes as far as he is able to go and still return home safely; the older child is restricted by physical ability (walking, cycling) and economic restraint (cost of bus); the adult in full command of faculties and with some economic independence has no real limitations except those of time and distance; and the aged are constrained by money and the deterioration of physical capacity and physical dynamics. The

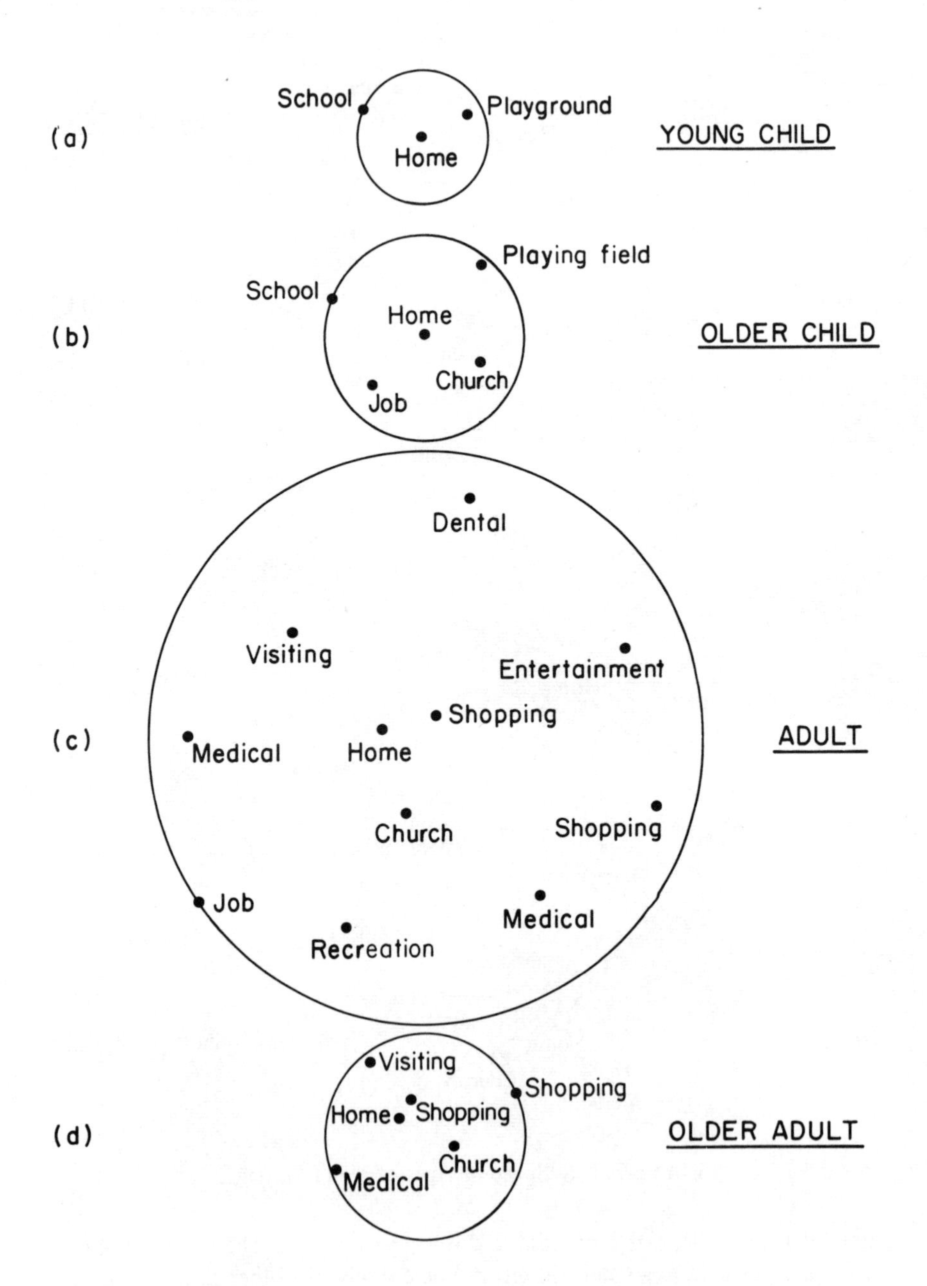

Figure 6-3. Life Space of Ages of Man (Radial)

handicapped, of course, are constrained much as are the elderly, with the added frustration, if they are younger, of difficult mobility for work and more youthful pursuits. All of these descriptions point the way toward improvement.

Greater Opportunity for the Young

The young may need money to be completely free of constraint upon their mobility, and the movement of affluent young in the United States in recent years must bear out the contention that, having the means, the young will find no constraints upon their mobility. But major concerns are (1) the poor young and rural (poor) young, and (2) that the young have *some place to go.*

In the first place, lack of funds as a constraint on youth particularly afflicts poverty areas, whether urban or rural, but most particularly rural areas, where distances are greater. The urban poor young can walk or cycle the short distances within which much opportunity exists (or should exist); the rural poor young cannot sympathize with the problem of preserving the 35 cent fare in New York City (as was recently a major demand), or of improving headways of buses from three minutes to two, when their costs may be counted in dollars, and headways measured in days.

Most incomprehensible are those situations where transportation to schools, at all levels, is inadequate. Transportation to school is an obvious necessity and must be provided at all levels and must be within the means of the student to pay for it.

The second aspect involves what the young person does at the other end of his trip. The lack or quality of social activity centers can be a major factor in the development of youth toward useful adulthood, or the avoidance of delinquency. This of course is beyond the scope of this book, but in this case transportation is merely the binding agent between home and activity, and the activity must, in quality and quantity, reflect social goals.

Do The Aged Want Greater Mobility?

While the facile response to this rhetorical question is that there is evidence to indicate that they do *not*, there is also evidence that "life space" and mobility in general are tied to too many other factors to answer in the affirmative for the elderly in general. Certainly there are natural restrictions in mobility as physical and mental powers diminish, as the circle of family and friends contracts. But another important consideration is the attitude of the elderly person towards the transport mode.

The differences in attitude toward transportation by various segments of society can be illustrated by considering the different vehicular users of the average city street. The private auto driver moves along a city street with a purpose, which may simply be to reach a destination at a specific time, or to find a parking spot. Unless he is late, he is under no pressure (except that of other traffic) to speed or to make sharp maneuvers.

The taxi driver, on the other hand, sees his driving as a job, and translates his time into money. He therefore shortens his driving time (and distance) by every means at his command, turning right from a left-hand lane, speeding and weaving in and out of traffic, stopping anywhere at or near a curb to pick up or discharge passengers. To the private auto driver, he is an impetuous, unpredictable, and downright dangerous driver.

The bus driver has a job which requires him to go from point *A* to point *B*, more or less on schedule. He is paid by the hour, not by how many passengers he carries, and he is paid whether he meets his schedule or not. Consequently, he will move along at the speed of traffic, he will bully smaller vehicle drivers by the sheer size of his own vehicle, he will pick up and discharge passengers in the middle of the street if it is most convenient, and he will generally ignore the constraints of time and speed under which his passengers may labor.

Thus each driver sees the other as a hazard and an inconvenience. In like manner the young see transportation as a necessity but one which can be essentially ignored, or vandalized, or littered. The adults see transportation as a necessity and one which must get them to work on time and be consistently reliable. The elderly see transportation as an experience along the way to another experience, and both should be leisurely and pleasurable. The handicapped see transportation as an absolute necessity and one which must be adapted to their special needs.

The conflicts in these views arise when youth is boisterous or rowdy amongst the serious adults; when the rush-hour adults are "impeded" by slow-moving elderly or handicapped; when the elderly are forced to use facilities that are inimical to them physically and/or psychologically; and when the handicapped are forced to use modes which charge exorbitant fees.

That the elderly may not want more mobility seems to be a conclusion of studies which have looked into the possibilities of enticing those house-bound elderly to go farther afield, whether alone or in groups. In such cases it may be that there is a greater psychological barrier to overcome than there is a physical barrier. Aged persons who have convinced themselves that it is a part of aging to be restricted in movement and mobility will be the most difficult to convince (after many years of reclusion) that they are quite capable of travel, even in its simplest forms.

With the majority of elderly, however, it is the gradual reductions in mental and physical acuity which demand adjustments in public modes of transportation. Knowledge of a transportation system, difficult to the normally alert, will be much more difficult to many aged. Signs and symbols will need greater clarity of explanation:

Time is a factor which needs adjustment to fit the capacities of the aged. The time it takes a subway train to load and unload at a station is decided by "average" values measured on "average" persons. These same "dwell times" must accommodate the slower aged and handicapped.

Distance is another factor to be considered. The distance to a mass transit facility may be considered reasonable for the majority of the population (again such figures are "average"), but it may be painfully difficult and time-consuming for the aged. Distances within facilities also are geared towards the physically capable majority. This is most painfully evident within airports, with their extremely long distances between terminals, from terminal area to airplane, etc. But bus and railroad terminals can also be designed with an insensitivity to such problems.

Cost is the major problem to the aged as it is to all of the economically disadvantaged. Half-fare programs are a decided advantage to the aged as long as transportation facilities are adequate in other respects to the needs of the aged. The reduced fare is useless if there is poor off-peak service (as is most generally the case with rapid transit and bus systems anxious to cut costs), causing long waits for the elderly under poor conditions of weather, comfort, or physical security.

Structural or mechanical inadequacies are perhaps the most obvious drawbacks to the use of public transportation by the elderly. The usual litany of "difficulties" can be recited. A listing from the 1969 Senate Report[7] includes:

1. Sheltered benches.
2. Subway gates.
3. No-step buses.
4. Well-spaced poles.
5. Computerized speeds.
6. Collecting fares.
7. One-way doors.

In this brief listing we can see examples of the major complaints which elderly (and other handicapped persons) have with mass transit. "Sheltered benches" suggests the need to provide locations where the elderly can wait in comfort for the bus (or the subway or the commuter train). But sheltered benches may not be enough. First of all, the big cities are plagued by vandalism and muggings. A shelter of any kind will fall prey to such social aberrants, and any users of such a shelter are in a dangerously secluded location lending itself to violence. It may be of greater importance to provide the knowledge concerning the transit facility (schedules, routes, fares, etc.) which minimizes the need to sit and wait on "sheltered benches." Weather conditions, in fact, may make it useless to provide unheated waiting areas for the elderly. But the provision of realistic schedules requires a tightening of operating procedure on the part of operating agencies which may be beyond their willingness and capability.

"Subway gates" deals with the problem of overcrowding on subway platforms, a condition that certainly frightens the elderly or handicapped person from taking part in the peak-hour fray of most big cities. And yet systems like the one in Paris can meter access to platforms so that trains are never overcrowded. But systems such as these are perhaps an expression of national or regional psychology rather than design intent. The phenomenon visible in New York subways today, wherein persons will board a train without permitting passengers to get off first, is of recent appearance. A general decline in concern for fellow men is apparent in the increase in filth in big cities, and attitudes, manners, and morals cannot be legislated. American subways are generally designed for their overcrowded condition and would not pay off too well at reasonable capacities. One hundred twenty passengers *per car* is considered to be a "comfortable" standing load, equivalent to track volumes of 48,000 passengers per hour, but track volumes have been measured at over 60,000.[8] Subway gates could control this demand and in the process make the commuter who misses his train, and the operating agency, unhappy. But the concept of subway gates could be pursued for application during off-peak hours, when it might even be of help in aiding the security problem.

"No-step buses" suggests the problem which is always first in the recitation of difficulties encountered by the aged and handicapped: the bus step is too high. Henry Perry told the story of when he "was riding a bus, and a gentleman . . . 79 years old . . . had a little box he carried with him. He had made himself a little step; he would put this little box down, get on the first step, reach down and pick it up and get on the bus."[9]

There are essentially two problems with bus steps: one involves their original design, which is based on that great "average" of the majority of population capabilities. Fruin, for instance, notes that "maximum riser heights should be 7 inches; preferred riser heights would be between 5 and 6 inches." And "a riser height increase of 37.5 percent, from 6 inches to 8.25 inches, resulted in an increase in energy cost of 96 percent in ascending, and 58 percent in descending."[10]

Certainly the problem is more than just energy expenditure for the elderly and handicapped. It is a matter also of physical capability for raising the foot 8 inches or 12 inches, or even 5 inches. How many persons would be aided by reducing step heights by one inch, or two, is one of the facts which need uncovering.

But the other serious problem with bus steps is the lack of consistency on the part of the driver as to where he opens his door: if he pulls in to the curb, the stair height (to the first, or lowest step) may be anywhere from 5 to 8 inches, generally, depending on the height of the curb, but if he opens his door anywhere *away* from the curb, because of traffic congestion, lack of maneuverability, laziness, or pure cussedness, the first (bottom) step is something more like 12 inches high or greater. This is not only difficult for the elderly, it is difficult (and dangerous) for the "normal" passenger. In this respect the bus system is less controllable than rapid-transit systems. Because of driver freedom and an almost limitless choice-decision capability, the patron is at the mercy of the driver.

The development of no-step buses is a possibility, of course. It is not yet common in city streets for a number of reasons. There must be a space between the bottom step and the street pavement; this is common sense (unless we consider the possibilities of retractable gear). If that space is minimal, say 2 inches, there are grave problems with designing a suspension for the bus. If the first step, or the floor of the bus, is designed to match the height of the curb, or the sidewalk, the problem emerges of the lack of consistency in curb heights, and the lack of permanence of such curb height even if they were consistent (the curb height changes each time the street is repaired or repaved).

It is not that it is impossible to develop a vehicle with low clearance (distance from street to bottom of vehicle), but the current and future expectable state of city streets, with ruts, potholes, uneven paving, remains of cobblestones, remaining trolley-car rails, etc., etc., make it rather difficult to envision. But the real solution lies with a look at the other form of mass transit: the train or subway. In this case the platform, from which the passenger steps to enter the vehicle, is high enough to be *on the same* level as the interior floor of the vehicle. In such a situation it is unimportant what the clearance of the vehicle is above the ground. What this concept requires of course, is either a general raising of all sidewalks in cities (or general lowering of all streets), or the construction of true bus stations where bus stops exist (besides the redesign of buses themselves). Such a solution would permit the elderly and handicapped to mount the platform at their own speed (using reasonably designed stairs and/or ramps), and enter the vehicle on a level plane.

"Well-spaced poles" refers to the difficulty of the elderly and handicapped have in mounting steps (in buses, especially), and then in maneuvering themselves, or just standing during a trip, within the vehicle. Handrails and poles must be designed to be helpful, meaning within reasonably short grasping distance, to those who cannot stretch their arms across long distances. Overhead bars, rails, or straps in trains and buses, may also be out of reach to the short, or the bent with age or physical impairment. Upright poles and waist-high railings should be placed in almost continuous profusion within the travel space of public vehicles, as an aid and comfort to all passengers, not only the aged or handicapped.

"Computerized speeds" is a feature related to the need for "well-spaced poles." It is perhaps a generalization to speak of "speeds"; what is meant here is the difficulty passengers have maintaining balance when the vehicle lurches during starting, slowing and stopping, or on turns. This is a matter related to two aspects of the transportation operation: the driver's proficiency (and mental attitude); and the vehicle's physical capabilities. Greatest difficulty is experienced during boarding and alighting: drivers will usually close the door (on a bus) and accelerate before all passengers have found their seats, or a convenient hold on a post. On alighting, a passenger must rise (if from a seat) before the bus stops, make his way to the exit, and await the opening of the door (some more recent buses add insult to injury by requiring the passenger to *push open* the rear door to exit). "Computerized speeds" is the forlorn hope that buses could be computerized insofar as acceleration, deceleration, and maneuvering. This hope is not an impossible one, but it requires even greater alteration of cityscapes than the earlier scenario described, or raised bus platforms for boarding and alighting. With this kind of requirement, we enter the world of automation. It is perhaps more reasonable to foresee new systems of "personal rapid transit," systems with their own exclusive rights of way, "capsules" which can be programmed to arrive at an individual's destination, with preprogrammed speeds, accelerations, and decelerations.

"Collecting fares" is a problem in that fares on buses are generally collected at the point of entry, while the bus may start up and disturb the passenger's balance the moment that he has his hands occupied with searching for change. The recent trend toward requiring exact fares on city buses has helped this situation, in that the fare can be held in hand before boarding and dropped in the fare box without excessive searching and counting. This, at least, is a *behavioral* adaption elderly passengers can make.

"One-way doors" refers to the deplorable tendency of passengers, mentioned earlier, of entering a vehicle while others are trying to leave it. If the front door of a bus were exclusively an entrance-way, and the rear door exclusively an exit, such problems could be eliminated. On trains, especially subway trains, this is more difficult. The system of gates discussed earlier might provide such a possibility, but simple designation of one door (of a car) as an entrance and one as an exit would hardly accomplish the desired result, even with a long period of public reeducation.

Another, unlisted area of major difficulty involves knowledge of transportation systems, schedules, fares and routes. The tendency in recent years for rapid-transit systems to cut down on nonpeak headways means long waits between trains in uncomfortable, unhealthy, and unsafe locations. No doubt schedules of such movements exist, but they are not publicized and easily available. With buses it is more difficult to know when to await a bus, since even with written and available schedules, bus movements will be sporadic and bunched.

As concerns other modes which can aid to improve the mobility of the elderly, some of the same arguments obtain. The "minibus" must be designed for ease of entrance and exit; it must have seats which are comfortable and safe; it must have a driver who understands the limitations of the elderly; and it must be reasonably priced (or free). Its great advantages, of course, are in its "door-to-door" aspect and its "demand-actuated" or "dial-a-ride" possibilities, because by these devices the elderly traveler need not walk to a public transit station or stop, need not negotiate with difficulty many stairs or a steep first step, need not wait in rain or cold or dark or dangerous surroundings for a vehicle.

The taxicab is used by the elderly a great deal, when they can afford it, for some of these very reasons, and it is not, by far, the ideal vehicle for this special group. Generally it is a late-model passenger car, with all of the drawbacks of low roof, tight rear seat, and difficulty of entrance and exit which are characteristic of late model cars. But it does come on demand, to the door, and takes one to his own specific destination.

Another recent listing of so-called "travel barriers" goes into greater detail (Table 6-1). Again, it is a matter of *physical* inadequacies, *information/directional* inadequacies, and *operational* inadequacies which make it difficult or impossible for the handicapped/elderly to use public transit.[11]

Some specific inadequacies have been related to specific population groups in Table 6-2. In such a breakdown, the relative value of various types of improvements can be calculated in a general way.[12]

Earning Enough to Pay for a Taxi (The Handicapped)

The difficulties enumerated as confronted by the elderly are those dealt with by the handicapped generally. In addition, it is the fairly youthful wheelchair-bound handicapped person who may find it necessary (and desirable psychologically) to have a job and work at it. Yet the city bus is completely beyond his capabilities, and the subway or train nearly so. Most such persons must find another mode, usually a private taxi, "car service," or limousine service, to commute to work (unless of course they are among the relative few who can drive specially equipped cars). And they find that most of their earnings, or at least an excessively major part of them, must go to pay the "fare" of such travel. This is the major problem for those handicapped not eligible or desirous of help either from a voluntary organization or the government. For these people it is of utmost importance that public transportation be adapted to their special needs.

Harold L. Willson, of the Kaiser Foundation Medical Care Program, in Oakland, California, himself confined to a wheelchair, waged an almost single-handed battle to have the then-planned BART (San Francisco Bay Area Rapid Transit) System modified to meet the needs of the elderly and handicapped. Shortly after the first beginnings of the system, Mr. Willson noted that no provision was being made to allow use by the elderly and handicapped, and therefore started a program to force the inclusion of such modifications. He did this by:

Table 6-1
Travel Barriers

Physical Barriers	Operational Barriers
VEHICLES	VEHICLES
High Step required to enter	Frequency of service
Difficult to get into or out of seats	Driver assistance/attitude
Seats not available/forced to stand	Acceleration/deceleration
Difficult to reach handholds	Information presentation
Cannot see out for landmarks	Schedules maintenance
No place to put packages	Inadequate or inappropriate routes
Cannot see or hear location information	Too many transfers
Nonvisible signs	
TERMINALS	TERMINALS
Long stairs	Employee assistance/attitude poor
Long walks	Information clarity and dissemination
Poor fare collection facilities	Length of stops too short
Poor posting of information	Crowd flow non-directed
Poor crowd flow design	Little or no interface with other modes
Insufficient seating	
Little interface with other modes	
TRANSIT STOPS	TRANSIT STOPS
Insufficient shelter	Poor location: for safety; for convenience
Platform incompatible with vehicle	Not enough stops
Inadequate posting of information	Information displayed insufficient or confusing

Source: *The Handicapped and Elderly Market for Urban Mass Transit*, Transportation Systems Center, U.S. Department of Transportation, Cambridge, Mass. NTIS PB 224 821, October 1973.

1. Getting support from elderly and handicapped individuals and organizations.
2. Convincing the BART direction and staff of the needs of the large group he represented.
3. Extracting a policy statement from the BART direction to permit a design which would permit addition of facilities at a later date, if necessary.
4. Obtaining funds and authority from the State Legislature for changes in the system.

Table 6-2
Handicap Class Related to Functional Requirements for Travel

Function	A	B	C	D	E	F	G
1. Walk or go more than one block				X		X	
2. Move in crowds	X		X	X	X	X	X
3. Stand or wait				X	X	X	
4. Board quickly	X		X	X	X	X	X
5. Climb shallow, short stairs			X	X			
6. Climb steep or long stairs			X	X	X	X	X
7. Use inclines				X			
8. Deposit exact fare	X			X	X	X	X
9. Maintain balance while standing in moving vehicle (with aid of pole, seat, etc.)			X	X	X	X	X
10. Sit down, stand up			X	X			
11. Respond to visual cues	X						
12. Respond to audio cues		X					

X means: Cannot perform function by self without substantial difficulty.

Handicap Class Identifiers and Numbers Affected

A. Visually Impaired (1,970,000
B. Deaf (330,000)
C. Uses Wheelchair (430,000)
D. Uses Walker (410,000)
E. Uses Other Special Aids (5,470,000)
F. Other Mobility Limitation (3,310,000)
G. Acute Conditions (490,000)

Source: *The Handicapped and Elderly Market for Urban Mass Transit*, Transportation Systems Center, U.S. Department of Transportation, Cambridge, Mass. NTIS PB 224 821, October 1973.

The improvements Mr. Willson was successful in having added to the BART system include:

1. Elevators, equipped with telephone and controls within reach of wheelchair occupants.
2. Toilet facilities with appropriate door widths and handholds to permit use by elderly and handicapped.
3. Stairs with handrails extending beyond the top and bottom steps.
4. Special parking facilities with wider-than-usual stalls.
5. Modifications to the cars themselves to provide small spaces between platform and car, wide doors, and ease of movement within the car.
6. Combined loudspeaker directions and easily read signs; provisions for seeing-eye dogs and other help for the blind.
7. Special service gates and fare collection machinery, a closed-circuit television system, and special directional signs.

These are the modifications which must be included in new facilities; the difficulty is with the improvement of *existing* facilities. And the difficulty there is not so much in the physical problem of making such changes to old systems (although it is a formidable task), but in the *costs* involved. Existing transportation systems have problems just in meeting operating fund requirements; maintenance has gone downhill for many recent years.

7 Case Study: Can We Really Reduce Unemployment Through Transportation?

We have shown that the rate of unemployment among low-skilled workers can be related to the level of transportation available to them. On the basis of this calibrated model it is now possible to estimate the unemployment reduction attributable to transportation improvements.

To illustrate the application of the employment-accessibility model, we again make use of the data from the CBMC Transportation Study. The area selected for case study is located in Brownsville. The accessibility of this area, located south of Sutter Avenue, is the lowest of all areas in Central Brooklyn. This area contains 10,255 unskilled workers, of whom 2015 are non-hard-core unemployed.

Objectives

The objectives of this chapter are:

1. To illustrate the use of the model in a real-life application.
2. To show that the model produces results which facilitate decision-making.
3. To evaluate alternative plans.[a]

The first objective is actually accomplished by (2) and (3). The development of the second objective is as follows.

The Model as an Aid in Decision-Making

The work-trip mobility analysis contained in the CBMC Report resulted in the identification of employment zones in need of improved transportation service. Twelve such zones were identified, and they are shown in Figure 7-1. These zones represent the principal industrial areas of Brooklyn and Queens. They are within a 7.5-mile radius of Brownsville, and contain about 40,400 low-skilled jobs.

Table 7-1 identifies the employment zones, the number of low-skilled jobs located in each, their distance from Brownsville, and the travel time, using existing transit.

[a]Alternative plans *should include* some basically different systems; some variation of systems; and some combinations thereof, as appropriate.

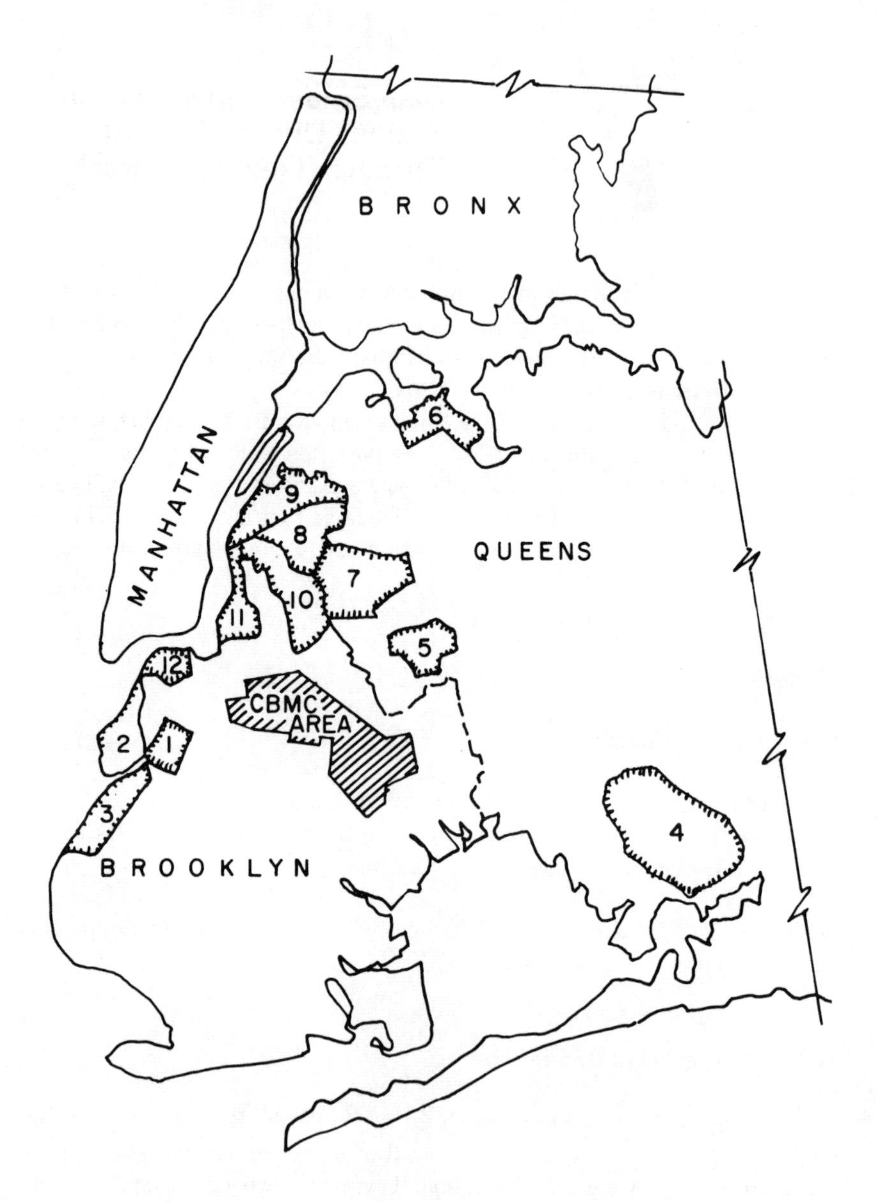

Figure 7-1. Low-Skilled Job Concentration in Brooklyn and Queens

Improvement of public transportation to these employment zones, which are widely dispersed, calls for a transit system which would connect individual origins to individual destinations. A limited "door-to-door" transit service[b] is

[b]"Door-to-door" transit service implies walking only *one* or *two* blocks, *from* the origin or *to* the final destination of the trip.

Table 7-1
Distribution of Low-Skilled Job Concentrations in Brooklyn and Queens

Area Identification	Identification of Employment Areas in Map 6-1	Total Low-Skilled Jobs	Air-line Distance from Brownsville	Travel Time via Existing Transit
Brooklyn				
Gowanus, Red Hook,	1	1630	4.8 miles	44 minutes
Bush Terminal	2	3159	5.7	50
	3	2967	6.2	49
Navy Yard &	11	2704	4.1	42
Greenpoint	12	5669	5.0	47
Newtown Creek	10	3960	2.7	48
Queens				
Ridgewood	5	441	2.5	43
Maspeth	7	1809	4.2	55
Woodside	8	484	4.6	62
Long Island City	9	7028	5.7	50
LaGuardia Airport	6	1049	7.5	83
JFK Airport	4	4605	6.8	62

most appropriate for this purpose. Three levels of door-to-door service will be tested as possible alternative improvements. These are referred to as the *maximum*, the *intermediate*, and the *minimum* plans.

The *maximum* plan is the most flexible of the three, because it calls for the most individually exclusive service. The residential area is divided into three pickup zones, each with its own vehicles, and workers are then transported *directly*, without stopping en route, to the zone of employment common to all occupants of the vehicle. This plan allows for a total of 36 (3 x 12) mutually exclusive trip combinations.

The *intermediate* plan is similar to the maximum plan except that travel routes are established. This plan permits delaying a passenger destined to zone (n) to discharge a passenger in zone (n-1). The routes used in the intermediate plan are shown in Figure 7-2.

The minimum plan, like the intermediate plan, also makes use of routes. This plan, however, considers the entire area as *one* pickup zone, and further delays the passenger by forcing him to travel along while the driver completes the last pickup in the area.

Each of the three plans discussed above represents an improvement in travel time over the existing transit system. Of the three plans, the lowest travel time is achieved by the maximum plan, and the highest by the minimum plan. Table 7-2 shows the travel times for each of the three plans, and also shows the existing conditions (the "Do-Nothing Alternative").

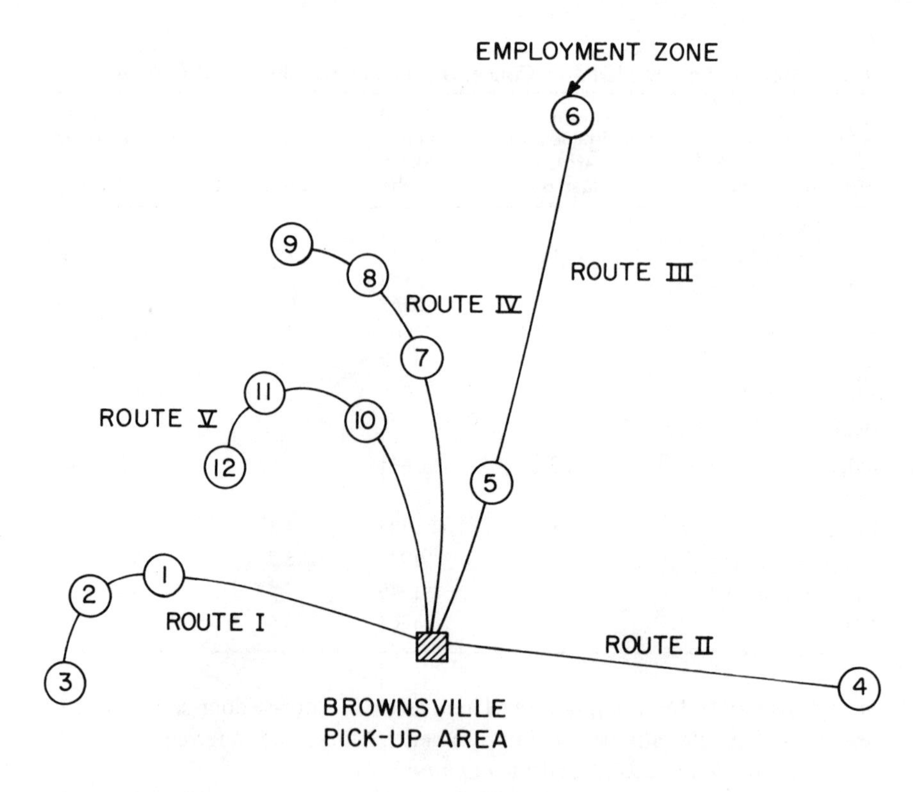

Figure 7-2. Intermediate Plan: Door-to-Door Transit System

Changes in Unemployment Due to Changes in Accessibility

The changes in unemployment for a given residential area can be determined by a change in any of the following conditions:

1. Transportation service to employment zones.
2. The number of jobs located in the employment zones.
3. Both transportation service and jobs.

For the purpose of this study, it is estimated that only a change in transportation service can be expected in the short run. If the jobs available in an area also were to change, however, it would be easy to incorporate this occurrence in the model.

The employment-accessibility model was described mathematically as:

$$Y_i = 186.26 - 31.65 \log_{10} X_i \tag{7.1}$$

Table 7-2
Travel Times from Brownsville to Employment Zones

	Zones of Employment											
Alternatives	1	2	3	4	5	6	7	8	9	10	11	12
"Do-nothing" plan	44	50	49	62	43	83	55	62	50	48	42	47
Maximum plan	30	34	23	30	20	49	31	35	36	23	25	28
Intermediate plan	30	39	45	30	20	54	31	40	45	23	35	43
Minimum plan	35	44	49	35	25	59	36	45	50	28	40	47

where

Y_i = the unemployment rate in a residential zone (in percent) and
X_i = the residential accessibility index of the residential zone
= $\Sigma E_j F_{ij}$

A change in unemployment from an initial condition, Y_{i0}, to a new condition resulting from transportation improvements, Y_{it}, may be represented as:

$$\Delta Y_i = Y_{i0} = 31.65 \ (\log_{10} X_{it} - \log_{10} X_{i0}) \tag{7.2}$$

this is illustrated below.

It is possible, then, to assess the impact of transportation improvements on the unemployment levels in Brownsville. Improvements in transportation service, between parts of Brownsville and the job sites located in Brooklyn and Queens, will mean reduced travel times. A lower travel time is, in turn, translated into a higher accessibility by the relationship:

$$X_i = \Sigma E_j F_{ij} \tag{7.3}$$

where F_{ij} is a function of travel time (see Figure 5-3).

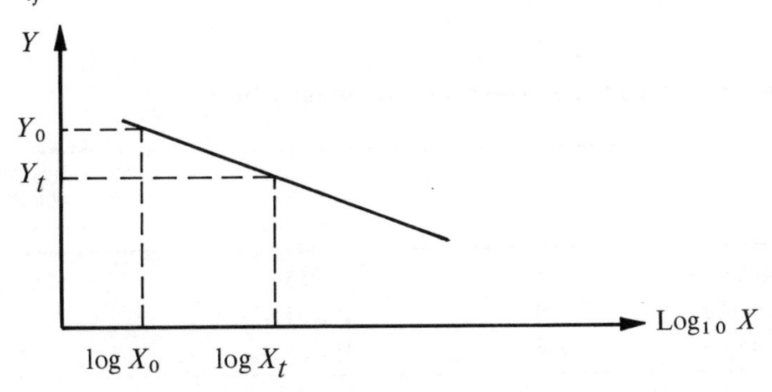

The new accessibilities of each plan may be calculated from the following relationship:

$$X_{At} = X_{A0} + \sum_{j=1}^{12} E_j (F_{Ajt} - F_{Aj0}) \tag{7.4}$$

where:

X_{At} = New accessibility index for area A
X_{Ao} = Old accessibility index for area A
j = An employment zone with improved transportation access
F_{jt} = The travel-time factor from area A to employment zone j resulting from the proposed transportation improvements
F_{Ajo} = Old travel-time factor from area A to employment zone j.

The quantity $\sum_{j=1}^{12} (F_{Ajt} - F_{Aj0})$ is calculated for each plan in Tables A-1 through A-5 of Appendix A. The new accessibilities resulting from the maximum, intermediate, and minimum plans are computed from Equation (7.4):

$$X_A \text{(maximum plan)} = 180{,}000 + 19{,}355 = 199{,}355$$

$$X_A \text{(intermediate plan)} = 180{,}000 + 10{,}564 = 190{,}564$$

$$X_A \text{(minimum plan)} = 180{,}000 + 5{,}918 = 185{,}918$$

Substituting these values into Equation (7.2) yields the *reduction* in the unemployment rate caused by the increase in transportation accessibility. In this way, the number of low-skilled workers who will become employed can be calculated. This is summarized in Table 7-3 for each plan.

Table 7-3
Projected Employment Resulting from Accessibility Increases

Plan Alternatives	ΔY_A	Low-Skilled Labor Force	Number of Workers Who Will Become Employed
Maximum plan	1.58%	10,255	162
Intemediate plan	0.95%	10,255	97
Minimum plan	0.63%	10,255	65

Cost-Effectiveness

These results show that, although the number of workers who will become employed is significant, especially for the maximum plan, the effectiveness of a door-to-door transit system is minimal in lowering the unemployment *rate* in the area.

Whether or not it is justifiable to implement any of the alternative plans, however, depends on their cost and the benefits which they provide. Although the cost of each alternative plan can be readily estimated, the benefits brought about by these plans are difficult to estimate precisely. For this purpose, it is assumed that the income earned by a low-skilled worker can be interpreted as *the social benefits accruing to society for foregoing the public support of the unemployed worker.* An annual income of $4,160.00 (corresponding to an hourly wage of $2.00) is used in this analysis. For the 162 workers employed through the maximum plan, the total annual benefit amounts to $673,920.00; the intermediate plan produces a benefit of $403,520; and the minimum plan yields a benefit of $270,400.

To estimate the cost of each plan, it is necessary to know the vehicle requirements as well as the amount of travel. Determining the number and type of vehicles needed to transport the newly employed workers depends on the demand volume which requires the service. The demand volume consists of *two* components:

1. The work trips of the newly employed.
2. The work trips of those who *currently* travel to the areas of employment receiving transportation improvements.

This latter group should be included in the demand volume because the improved service, which is more direct and more convenient,[c] will attract travelers from other transit routes which serve the existing travel demand.

For the newly employed, the demand volume between Brownsville and each employment zone is estimated with the Gravity Model method of trip distribution. Trip interchange calculations for each of the three plans are shown in Tables B-1, B-2, and B-3 of Appendix B. The *existing* travel to each employment zone is calculated from the origin-destination (O-D) data of the CBMC Study.

Table B-4 of Appendix B summarizes the existing travel between Brownsville and each of the 12 employment zones. It will be noted that the *existing* travel demand is *larger* than the projected demand generated by the improved accessibility to the twelve employment areas. In this case then, the number of vehicles which is necessary to implement an alternative plan far exceeds that which is required to transport *only* the newly employed workers. The cost factor, therefore, will increase without corresponding benefits.

---

[c]The fare is assumed at 35 cents per trip (the same as the New York City transit fare).

The *combined* travel demand on *each* of the three alternative plans is shown in Tables B-5, B-6, and B-7 of Appendix B. For each of the plans, the numbers and types of vehicles are determined by this total demand, and cost estimates are developed (see Appendix B).

The selection of the best plan for implementation (including the "do-nothing" alternative) is based on the criterion of *least total* cost to the government. The components of total costs are the subsidy of transit service and the cost of other public subsidy. These costs are tabulated in Table 7-4 and plotted in Figure 7-3. From these comparisons, the *intermediate plan* emerges as the *least costly plan.*

Decision-Making Under Uncertainty: The Demonstration Project

The decision process which has selected the *intermediate* plan as the best of the four alternatives considered, does not account for the fact that the employment-accessibility model is a probabilistic model. Cognizance of this fact, however, is vital for the success of a demonstration project. The purpose of a demonstration project is to "test" whether or not a certain "theory" works. The "proof" consists of providing tangible evidence (i.e., that people will become employed) to the decision-maker, so that he will become "convinced" that improving transportation accessibility will reduce unemployment. This objective, however, *may not* be best achieved if the *intermediate* plan is used in Brownsville.

For any given X (the independent accessibility variable) the individual values of Y (the dependent unemployment variable) are scattered above and below the regression line due to random disturbances. The employment-accessibility model predicts the *mean* value of the unemployment rate Y which corresponds to a given accessibility index. For a particular demonstration site, however, it is of interest to know how closely an *individual* value of Y can be predicted, rather

Table 7-4
Cost Effectiveness of Door-To-Door Transportation Improvements

Alternative	Expected No. of Workers Becoming Employed	Annual Income Earned	Cost to Government: Unemployment Subsidy	Cost to Government: Transit Subsidy	Expected Total Cost to Government
Maximum plan	162	673,920	0	549,930	549,930
Intermediate plan	97	403,520	270,400	274,275	544,675
Minimum plan	65	270,400	403,920	192,850	596,770
Do-nothing plan	0	0	673,920	0	673,920

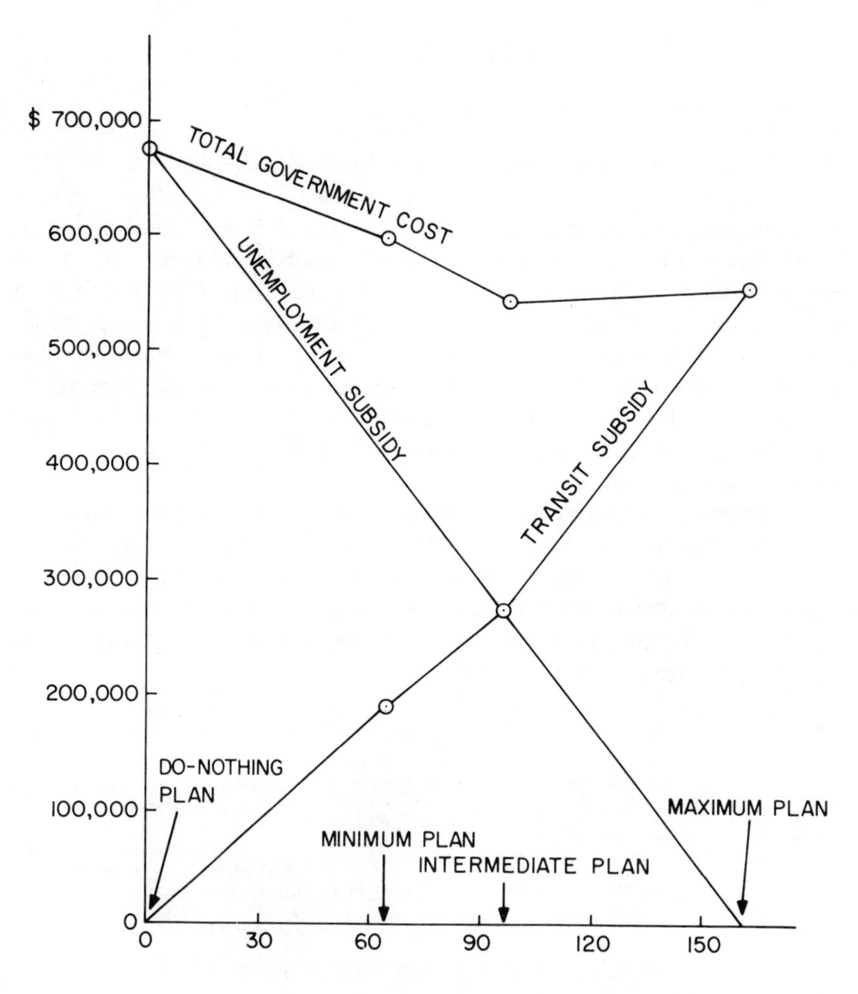

Figure 7-3. Cost Effectiveness of Alternative Plans

than to calculate the mean value of the regression line, which gives the best estimate of unemployment when many sites are concerned. This concept is discussed below.

Prediction Interval for Individual Value of Y

The prediction interval for Y is given by:

$$\hat{Y} \pm (t_{\alpha/2}, n\text{-}2)\, S_{y \cdot x} \sqrt{1 + \frac{1}{n} + \frac{(X - \bar{X})^2}{(n\text{-}1)\, S_X^{\,2}}} \tag{7.5}$$

where $\hat{Y}$ is calculated by the model, and α is the confidence level.

It is clear then, that calculating an expected unemployment reduction for *one* particular area does not guarantee that the expected Y will indeed occur, but rather that area (i) may have a Y_i falling in range $\hat{Y}\pm$ interval, 100 $(1 - \alpha)$ percent of the time. What this means is that it is possible to *detect no reduction* in unemployment whatsoever for a particular area, *even when transportation improvements are made.* The likelihood of detecting an improvement generally increases, however, as the size of the unemployment reduction increases. In general, the uncertainty of no improvement actually being detected is highest when the amount of unemployment reduction is very small. This concept is illustrated in Figure 7-4.

The shaded areas (degree of overlap) of cases (a) and (b) represent situations in which improvements may not be detected. The amount of overlap is seen to decrease as the size of unemployment reduction varies from small to large. This example shows that if the expected unemployment reduction were to exceed 5.28 percent, the uncertainty of detecting an improvement of this size would be zero at the 5 percent confidence level:

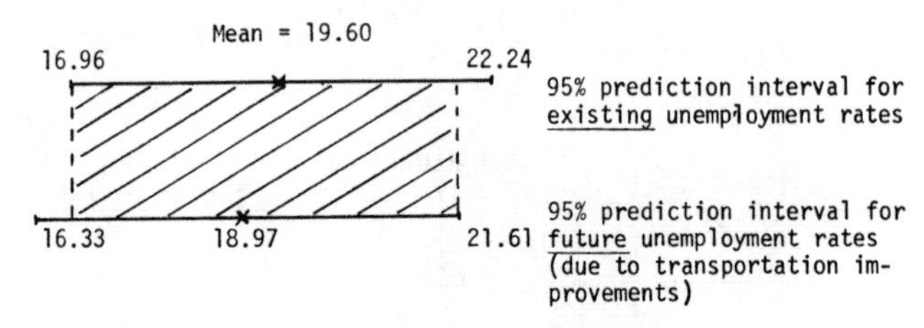

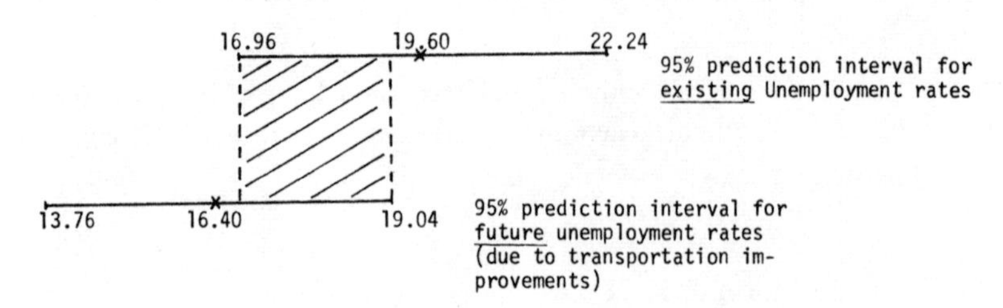

Figure 7-4. Uncertainty of Detecting A Reduction in the Unemployment Rate of an Area

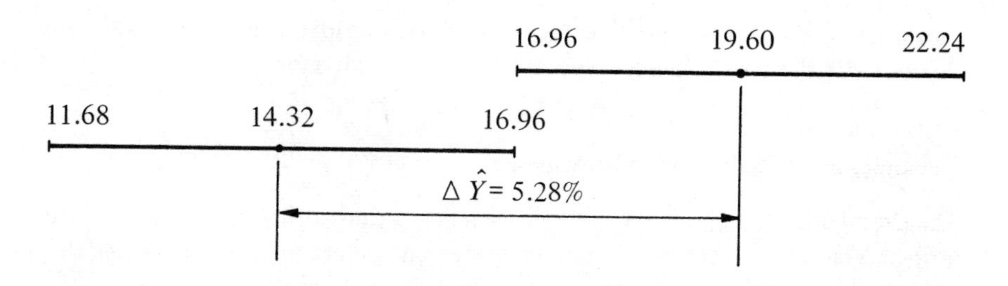

It is possible to estimate the amount of uncertainty, or the probability of failing to detect an improvement, by calculating the conditional probability of falling in the joint sample space of the existing and future unemployment distributions. This is shown in Figure 7-5.

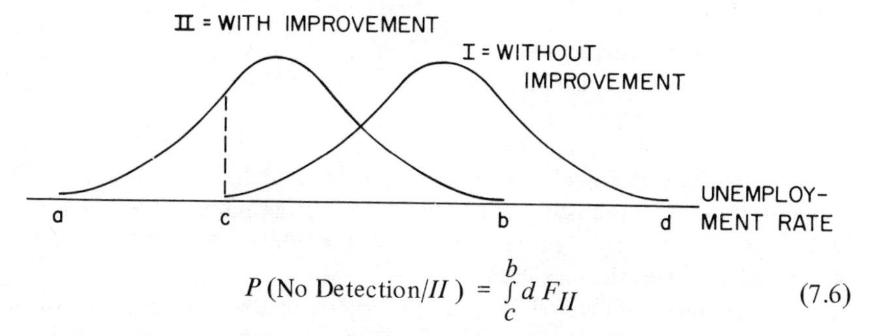

$$P\,(\text{No Detection}/II\,) = \int_c^b d\,F_{II} \qquad (7.6)$$

Figure 7-5. Probability of Not Detecting Unemployment Reduction, Given a Transportation Improvement

The probability of no detection is calculated by Equation 7.6

Characteristics of the Prediction Interval

Referring to Equation 7.2, it should be noted that the prediction interval is not uniform over the range of the independent variable, but in fact it is smallest when $X = \overline{X}$ and largest when X approaches the upper or lower limit of the

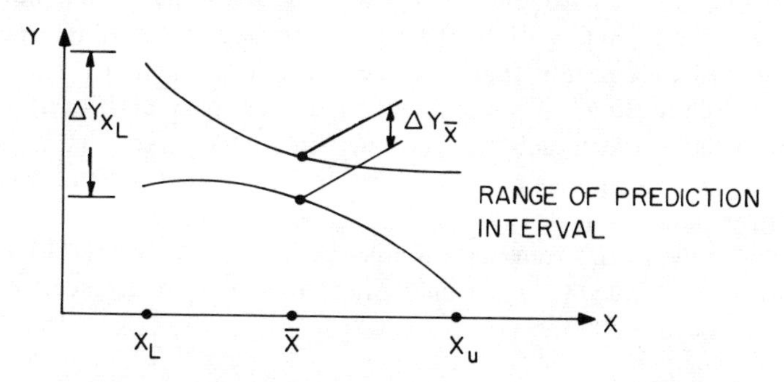

Figure 7-6. Prediction Interval for Individual *Y* Value.

range, i.e., $(X - \bar{X})$ is large (see Figure 7-6). This property has to be taken into account; for the case at hand, however, it is not a significant factor.

Unemployment Reduction in Brownsville

The Door-to-Door transportation improvements proposed for Brownsville should now be evaluated in terms of the unemployment detection criterion. When this is done for each of the three alternatives, the following results occur:

Alternative	Probability of *Not Detecting* a Reduction in Unemployment
Maximum plan	0.81
Intermediate plan	0.88
Minimum plan	0.90

These results indicate the futility of recommending the intermediate plan for demonstration. The probability of failing to detect an improvement under this plan is much too high. In fact, *none* of the three alternatives should be considered; not even the maximum plan.

The importance of these findings cannot be overstated. In fact they strongly suggest the cause for the "nonresults" of recent demonstration projects.

It is apparent that the selection of the least-cost plan among a set of test plans does *not* necessarily imply that the planner has succeeded in identifying the best plan for implementation. He has only been able to select the "best" of the array of plans which he is proposing. As it occurred in the above case, it is possible that *none* of the plans considered for evaluation represents a feasible alternative. It is obvious, then, that for Brownsville, the proposed plans must be supplemented or substituted with *additional* transportation improvements to have at least a 50-50 chance of detection.

A feasible alternate to the door-to-door system which could be used in improving the accessibility of Brownsville, consists of reducing the travel time from that area to a nearby transportation centroid, located at the junction of Broadway, Fulton Street, Atlantic Avenue, and East New York Avenue. At this junction, where several subway and bus lines meet (see Figure 7-7), the accessibility to employment areas is much higher than in Brownsville (the accessibility indices are 357,000 and 180,000, respectively). The travel time from Brownsville to this transportation centroid is approximately 30 minutes—even though it is located only 1.5 miles away (over-the-road distance)![1]

Figure 7-7. Transit Access to Transportation Centroid

A considerable reduction in travel time can be achieved if an *express shuttle* service is in operation. At an average peak-hour travel speed of twelve miles per hour, this distance could be covered in eight minutes. Assuming that an average of *four* minutes will be spent in walking to the express shuttle pickup points, the total travel time between Brownsville and the transportation centroid would be twelve minutes. On this basis, the new accessibility index for the area increases to 221,700 (see Appendix C). From Equation 5.4 this improvement is translated to an estimated unemployment of 16.25 percent:

$$Y_{At} = 186.26 - 31.65 \log 221{,}700 = 16.25$$

which represents a reduction of 3.36 percent over the existing level

(19.61 – 16.25 percent). The proposed improvement, therefore, results in the employment of 334 low-income workers (10,255 x 0.0336); this is more than twice the number estimated for the maximum plan for the door-to-door concept described earlier. To transport this volume during a sixty-minute A.M. peak period, a total of six minibuses is required operating at a four-minute headway. As was discussed earlier, however, this new service will attract, to the transportation centroid, travelers who now use other means of transportation. Additional capacity, then, has to be provided to transport about 2700 travelers from Brownsville to the transportation centroid. This results in a total demand of 3034 trips to be served by the proposed shuttle express. The required fleet size for this service is calculated at sixteen standard buses, operating at a ninety-second headway. The cost estimates for providing this service are shown in Appendix D.

The resulting benefits and costs of this service are shown in Table 7-5.

The net benefits accruing to the express shuttle service far exceed those of the maximum, intermediate, or minimum door-to-door transit systems (see Table 7-4) described earlier. It should be noted, however, that the express shuttle system and the door-to-door system can also be used in combination to provide varying levels of accessibility gains in Brownsville. The two systems can be combined, because they are *independent.* A summary of possible alternatives and their cost-effectiveness is given in Table 7-6.

It should be noted that Alternative 4, the express shuttle operation, has a much lower probability of "no detection" than any of the door-to-door alternatives. The *least-cost* solution, which is the combination of the express shuttle and the intermediate door-to-door system, has a very low risk of "no detection"; and the second more costly alternative, that which combines the express shuttle with the maximum door-to-door system, is shown to be the one with the highest probability of "success."

Using the criterion that a demonstration project should not be implemented unless there is at least a 50-50 chance that improvements can be detected, Alternatives 1 to 4 could be recommended. To insure the success of the demonstration project, Alternative 1 is recommended, since the incremental cost over the least-cost alternative is not significant, but the probability of success is increased considerably (0.80 vs. 0.70).

Table 7-5
Costs and Benefit of Express Shuttle Service to Transportation Centroid

Alternative Plan	Expected No. of Workers Becoming Employed	Annual Income Earned	Annual Cost of Service	Net Benefit
Express shuttle service	334	$1,389,440	$662,000	$727,440

Table 7-6
Cost-Effectiveness of Alternative Plans

Alternatives	Projected Reduction in Unemployment Rate (ΔY)	Expected No. of Workers Becoming Employed	Annual Income Earned	Cost of Subsidy		Expected Total Governmental Cost	Probability of No Detection
				Unemployment Subsidy	Transit Subsidy		
1. Express shuttle and maximum door-to-door	4.94%	496	$2,063,360	$ 0	$1,211,930	$1,211,930	0.20
2. Express shuttle and intermediate door-to-door	4.31	431	1,792,960	270,400	936,275	1,206,675	0.30
3. Express shuttle and minimum door-to-door	3.99	399	1,659,840	403,520	854,850	1,258,370	0.36
4. Express shuttle	3.36	334	1,389,440	673,920	662,000	1,335,920	0.48
5. Maximum door-to-door	1.58	162	673,920	1,389,440	549,930	1,939,370	0.81
6. Intermediate door-to-door	0.95	97	403,520	1,659,840	274,275	1,934,115	0.88
7. Minimum door-to-door	0.63	65	270,400	1,792,960	192,850	1,985,810	0.90
8. Do-nothing plan		0	0	2,063,360	0	2,063,360	1.00

Conclusions

The foregoing analysis demonstrates that each of the proposed improvements will not be self-supporting. In each of the alternatives tested, ridership revenues would cover less than five percent of the total system's cost. Even if this deficit were reduced by operating the vehicle during nonwork travel periods to serve other purposes, it is unlikely that fare revenues will rise even to fifty percent of the total annual cost.

The total cost-effectiveness of the proposed improvements are realized, however, when we account for the number of potential workers who will become employed, and consequently removed from public subsidy lists. Each of the alternatives foresees net savings when the costs of transit improvements are compared with the income earned by the newly employed workers. Transit subsidy is therefore *economically* justified for Brownsville.

Another important point must be made in justifying this subsidy. These vehicles could effectively be used in improving the delivery of needed services in the CBMC Area. These include travel to clinics, day-care centers, recreational and educational centers, and similar reasons. The need for such service was demonstrated by a study of taxi usage in the CBMC Area[2] which found that poverty household members constituted the largest group of taxi users. A more personalized transit system, therefore, could be established during off-peak hours with the radio-equipped vehicles of the proposed home-to-work transit improvements of Alternative 1. This secondary vehicle use would reduce the high travel costs of those who are currently taxi-captive.

The case study presented in this chapter has demonstrated that transportation improvements in an area, for the purpose of reducing its unemployment rate, should be carefully evaluated. Minimal improvements are not likely to succeed, because they are usually associated with a high probability of "no detection" (see Figure 7-4). It is important, moreover, to realize that using the transportation element as a means of reducing unemployment among low-skilled workers requires substantial public subsidies, since the improvements cannot be financed through the fare box. However, these improvements appear to be economically justified, because they tend to reduce the total costs of public subsidy to the unskilled worker. Finally, this case study has shown that although increases in transportation accessibility have projected the employment of a sizeable number of low-skilled workers, their maximum contribution (Alt. No. 1, Table 7-6) to lowering the rate of unemployment in the area was a change from an existing level of 19.6 percent, to a projected level of 14.7 percent.

It is apparent that even a very ambitious transit system improvement will not suffice to bring unemployment down to average levels.

This example has demonstrated that it is possible to improve the decision-making process beyond the level currently used in similar analyses for many cities throughout the United States. The utility of the unemployment-accessibility model for planning purposes rests primarily on its ability to estimate a more realistic expected level of improvement, avoiding the pitfalls encountered in recent demonstration programs. In addition, it guides the planner in selecting an improvement plan which most nearly meets the objectives of the potential demonstration and, perhaps more importantly, it will help him in eliminating proposals which are not expected to reduce unemployment to the level which would at least cover the costs of improvements. Finally, it permits a rational development of test plans to achieve varying levels of improvements. In this way the planner is able to evaluate the expected results from each proposal more rationally, thereby enabling him to make well-founded recommendations to the policy makers who must base their goals and objectives on what is technically possible *and* cost-effective.

8 Discussion: Can We Really Improve the Mobility of the Disadvantaged?

We have not developed a model for the testing of the cost-effectiveness of improvements in transportation provided to other elements of the transportation-disadvantaged for a number of reasons. For one, the provision of a link to a job, and thereby the provision of a job, is an easily measurable, objective value which lends itself to ease of manipulation. Cost of subsidy provided and subsidy avoided, also, are numerical and directly comparable. Where the difficulty arises is in the conversion of *subjective* values to numerical quantities, for purposes of comparison of cost-effectiveness. To some degree the Case Study of Chapter 7 had to confront this problem, but only peripherally.

For another, it may be that such a methodology is not needed in the same sense that a justification for a new bus line for the underemployed requires justification.

And yet, attempts at cost-benefit or cost-effectiveness in justifying a special service for the elderly/handicapped/youth have been made. They seem to follow the route of the justification of transportation safety measures: the cost of an improvement is rather clear-cut and straightforward (say the cost of straightening a section of roadway). The benefit accruable from the improvement is made up of many direct and indirect values:

1. The money saved by drivers in traffic transiting the section at a higher speed.
2. The money saved by the police/medical services in not having to respond to as many accidents.
3. The money saved by state or township in maintenance by not having to replace railings, lightpoles and such.
4. The money saved by drivers in not having wrecked vehicles.
5. The money saved by drivers/passengers in medical bills.
6. The money saved by insurance companies.
7. The money earned in a continuing lifetime of gainful employment.

It is apparent that only the money saved by police/medical teams, and money saved in direct repair (maintenance) costs are comparable to the cost of the improvement. The other amounts are imaginary, or individual, or ephemeral and arbitrary.

In similar manner we noted the calculation of benefits for the Raleigh County rural free bus system:

Transportation savings	($26,880)
Public sector goods and services	24,481
Shopping cost savings	7,680
Value of more trips taken	6,252
Health care	1,600
Bus system employee salaries	28,899
System operator profits	3,874
Loss of revenue profits by ad hoc operators	26,483
Store owner net income	1,536
Value added through multiplier effect	16,844
Total net benefits	$91,563[1]

Items such as "shopping cost savings," "value of more trips taken," "health care," etc., must spring from subjective judgments.

In assessing the value of these projects, in fact, government funding agencies have essentially sought *self-sufficiency*. Self-sufficiency may, indeed, be an unreasonable goal, a conclusion we can reach as we review "successful" and "unsuccessful" ventures alike. Reasonable fares today can only cover a rather small percentage of operating costs (much less of total costs) and subsidy is the only answer. It is certainly possible to show a net "profit" when we include subjectively arrived-at dollar totals and benefits to individuals; it is their overall *meaning*, to agencies and individuals alike, which can be questioned. Costs are usually clear-cut; benefits may not be. The question arises: how necessary is it to justify the existence and continuation of such projects on a cost-benefit or cost-effectiveness basis?

Ledger balances, then, will not determine the viability of these services. While a methodology can be developed, similar to the one in Chapter 6 for the underemployed, the results of systems developed for the young, the old, and the handicapped of this country must be rated on another scale, one which recognizes a need to bring the "fringe" groups of society into closer relationship to, and participation with, the majority. How, then, to improve the mobility of the disadvantaged? It appears that three factors are of utmost importance:

1. Drawing up a plan.
2. Marketing a service.
3. Confronting the "establishment(s)."

Drawing Up a Plan

Any transportation service intended to be of use to a specific group deserves proper preparation, in the form of data collection and analysis to determine the extent and character of patron participation, and to help determine proper routing and scheduling and operating procedures. The essential data appears to be

1. Demographic.
2. Attitudinal.
3. Physical/geographic.

Demographic data must include age, sex, and household information, but it must be extended to the collection of information on ethnicity, travel habits, travel purpose, activity schedules, location of friends and relatives, etc.

Attitudinal factors of importance concern the spirit of the proposed clientele: stay-at-homes require more than available transport to be drawn out. Measures of *anomie* (see Robinson and Shaver,[2] Thursz,[3] Fellman,[4] Stokol,[5] and Colong[6]) can be helpful in determining the plausibility of expecting participation by specific individuals.

Physical/Geographical considerations concern the area in which the transport is to operate; the existence of other modes of transportation, the physical barriers to their use and to use of the new mode, etc.

Marketing a Service

Marketing is a major part of the introduction and sale (acceptance) of a new transportation system. Transit-dependent groups will, in preservice interview, indicate general interest in a new system, and even indicate an intention to utilize it, but in confrontation with reality may avoid it in droves. Certainly where choices are clear-cut, substituting a free service for a fare-collecting one (as in Raleigh County) can be expected to have "success."

But of greatest importance is the need for developing a core clientele, a subscription clientele, which determines the minimum extent of the operation to come.

Confronting the "Establishment(s)"

The effort of Harold Willson[7] to convince the developers of the BART mass transportation system to provide accommodation for the elderly and handicapped is perhaps the classic confrontation. The effort to change attitudes on the part of the planners, designers, builders, and operators of transportation facilities is a continuing one. It goes beyond rapid transit systems. Efforts must be mounted towards:

Vehicle designers to consider the lesser capabilities of large segments of the public. Buses are continuously replaced in all city and rural systems. Generally the new ones are similar to the old ones in all those aspects which affect the comfort and basic requirements of the disadvantaged. Taxis are difficult to use by the young and supple, much less the older and handicapped. Pressures on vehicle manufacturers, on private fleet owners, and on licensing agencies must be developed.

Roadway designers to consider more than the vehicle. The pedestrian and the bicyclist must claim a larger share of the ownership of city streets, and crossing provisions must not be geared to the "average" man. Rest areas and safety refuges must have greater importance.

Terminal designers have developed a bare-bones, arid "style" which affects people's psyches deleteriously, which makes permanent some major difficulties for the weak, the aged, the slow, and the mentally deficient, and which lacks in humanity and concern for all users. Distances, means of rising from level to level, information dissemination, all must be rethought to avoid the anxiety experienced by most in terminal buildings, and especially by the disadvantaged.

Operators of systems must be convinced that there is a greater purpose than making money or being "efficient" at the expense of all but the great "average" population. Courtesy, helpfulness, consideration must return not only to public facilities but to official policy.

Unemployment and Transportation

A Restatement of the Problem

The approach which is typically followed for improving the transportation accessibility of a low-income area consists of setting up new bus routes to connect low-income areas to employment concentrations not well served by the regularly scheduled transit system.

The characteristic results produced by several deemonstration projects were illustrated in Chapter 4 using the Los Angeles and Long Island experiments. It was shown that the concepts which guided the implementation of these demonstration projects were not well specified, and, in fact, were largely dependent on trial-and-error experimentation. These efforts were largely inconclusive. Some bus routes were classified as successful and many others as failures. The common criterion used for evaluation was the *ridership* which was generated over an extended period of time (usually one year).

The problems quickly emerged from the analysis of these proposals. One involves *planning and management deficiencies* in properly identifying the relevant project variables; the other involves a *technological deficiency*. The nature of the first problem was the failure to identify the kind of *operational* objectives which would *measure* the degree of attainment of the project's goal, i.e., improving employment opportunities. The second problem dealt with the lack of an analytical measure which would relate a transportation improvement to an estimate of unemployment reduction. Since the costs associated with the implementation of a new transit system or improvement are very high, the inability of predicting the expected impact of an improvement often results not only in the adoption of a poor plan, but also in a waste of public funds.

Planning and Management Deficiencies

The main issue which continually emerges from a review of the literature on the subject is the general lack of definition and identification of criteria which could be used in evaluating the outcome of a project. Invariably only one concept is employed in characterizing the success or failure of an experimental bus line: passenger revenue and operating costs. Bus lines whose revenues did not cover their cost of operation were either dropped or consolidated at the end of the demonstration period. This was done without regard to their ridership composition: i.e., the following questions were not answered: How many riders *became employed* as a result of the newly installed service; *or*, how many persons who were no longer bus riders did, in fact, obtain initial employment because of the bus line but *were later traveling by automobile?*

Perhaps the lack of this information indicates not only a failure in properly defining the project's objectives but, more significantly, it may reflect the initial uncertainties faced by the planners when confronted with the task of developing transit service routes. Among other areas not covered are the following:

1. Design of elaborate checks to identify every project bus rider with respect to his employment history, mode of travel prior to using the project bus, and what became of him if he no longer used the project bus, i.e., did he stop working or did he subsequently buy a car for traveling to work?
2. Differentiation between hard-core and non-hard-core unemployment, to sort out the unemployed who require special programs in addition to transportation improvements to induce them to work.
3. Determination of whether the new service was sufficient in scope to significantly reduce the inaccessibility of an area. The meaning of this was pointed out in Chapter 7, where it was shown that minimal improvements have a high probability of not being detected.
4. Testing independent alternative plans for the purpose of selecting the best plan for implementation.

While the first two items would have been possible to accomplish, the second and third items could not be realized because there was no method by which to quantify the relationships of transportation improvements and unemployment among low-income workers. This important gap has been filled by the work presented in this book. It is now possible to develop more rational plans by obtaining estimates of expected results from a number of potential alternatives *before* the implementation of a plan, and avoiding unnecessary expenses.

Cautions and Model Sensitivity

In applying the model to the case study of Chapter 7, it was assumed that potential employment areas contained job openings to satisfy the number of unskilled workers distributed there by the Gravity Model. This should be subject to verification in practice, and, in fact, job openings data should be substituted for the total employment as the attraction of an employment area.

Throughout the foregoing analyses and discussions it was assumed that the total job vacancies in New York City were at least equal to the number of unemployed. If this were not the case, the potential benefits of transportation improvements would not be fully realized.

It should be noted, in addition, that the potential reduction in unemployment attributable to higher accessibility is related to the observed differentials between zones of lowest and highest accessibility. As shown in Figure 5-11, the minimum unemployment rate that could be achieved in a zone of poorest accessibility would not go below 8.5 percent (19.6 – 11.1). For the CBMC Area it was found that the marginal reduction in unemployment decreases at a slower rate for zones of higher accessibility, and when the accessibility index of 420,000 is exceeded, the marginal reduction approaches zero. Thus it appears that the elasticity of the model is highest when the initial accessibility conditions are poorest and it becomes inelastic as the accessibility of a zone approaches 420,000 units. The implication of this observation is the apparent conclusion that lack of adequate transportation in the CBMC Area can explain up to approximately 56 percent (11.1 ÷ 19.6) of the total unskilled unemployment (see Figure 5-11).

The model is restricted in its application to zones whose accessibility indices fall in the range of calibration. This restriction, however, does not appear to be a serious one for the CBMC Area since a transportation improvement in a zone of low accessibility is not likely to increase the accessibility of that zone beyond the upper range of calibration. Furthermore, any improvements made in zones of high accessibility can be assumed to produce insignificant unemployment reduction since the model is highly inelastic at the upper range of calibration.

As shown in Chapter 7, the sensitivity of the model to transportation improvements is quite low, i.e., what appeared to be significant transportation improvements produced minimal gains in unemployment reduction. For example, the minimum Door-to-Door alternative plan (which required an investment of *eight* medium-size buses and *one* 14-seat Ford-type Econoline) projected an expected reduction in unemployment of 0.63 percent (or 65 workers). In addition, the probability of *not* detecting any improvement was high (0.90)—a crucial consideration for a demonstration project.

Without this information, the plan might have been implemented with high expectations but without any basis for having the possibility of any success being detected. In this case an additional inconclusive finding might have been reported. So, one important point made in Chapter 7 was the realization that small plans will not be effective, and that in order to use transportation as a tool for reducing unemployment, the degree of improvement must be substantial. It is perhaps largely due to this phenomenon that the experiments in Los Angeles and Long Island did not confirm the effectiveness of the transportation element.

Applicability of the Model in Other Areas

Although the accessibility-employment model in its present form is limited in use for the CBMC Area, its conceptual development and structure should *not* vary from area to area. Thus the same approach can be replicated in another city.

The components of the model are:

1. Transit travel times.
2. Employment concentrations.
3. Unemployment rates.
4. Travel time factors.

The first two are relatively easy to obtain at minimum cost. Transit travel times can be calculated from a knowledge of transit routes, service headways, and roadway speeds. Employment concentrations can be estimated from federal and state bureaus of labor statistics data or regional employment data banks kept by a planning agency or commercial associations.

From the discussions of Chapter 5, a comprehensive survey of unemployment conditions in the area should be undertaken. Determination should be made in clarifying the unemployed between hard-core and non-hard-core. The historical frequency of unemployment and its duration should prove to be helpful in this regard. A home interview survey would be helpful in this task as well as in the analysis of the work trip distribution for unskilled workers. This latter information is required for the travel time factors ($F_{i\text{-}j}$'s) needed for the calculation of accessibility indices. This is all that is required for *calibrating* the model. The process of implementation, however, requires more specific data on the number of job openings in an employment area. This information may be obtained through state and city employment offices and/or by actual employer interviews. Either of these two tasks are time consuming, and require skilled personnel to perform them.

Data Sources for Model Calibration

The type of data required for model calibration and transit system improvements is usually available from a number of sources. These include:

1. Transportation studies.
2. Welfare agencies.
3. State employment agencies.
4. U.S. census.

Transportation Studies

Home Interview Files. The Home Interview file contains data items which include socioeconomic data, car ownership, occupation of residents, employment classification, trip data stratified by purpose and mode, and destinations of trips made by the household's residents. The purpose of this data would be to establish the travel pattern profiles of the low-income workers and to determine their location within the study area. It is likely, however, that the sample size of the traffic zones is not large enough to contain adequate representation of low-income households.

Land Use File. The land in the urbanized area is classified into 99 categories, by traffic zone. This classification would permit the identification of employment areas particularly suitable for low-income employment, i.e., industrial, commercial, and institutional.

Transportation Facilities. The highway and transit systems serving the urbanized area are fully described in terms of capacity, speed, and transit headways. Transit companies are an additional source.

These data sources are readily accessible and are sufficient for calibrating the travel time factors (F_{i-j}'s) of the low-skilled home-to-work travel.

Welfare Agencies

File on Aid to Families with Dependent Children (AFDC). This file contains detailed information on household size, location of household, employability, transportation and other services. Because of the obvious incentive to register, this file would contain virtually a 100 percent sample of all families in the study area eligible for assistance. It is very difficult, and practically impossible, to have access to this file, for reasons related to the protection of individual privacy.

State Employment Data

Data on employment statistics is published periodically primarily by political areal units. Occasionally smaller area summaries are provided when special studies are made. These reports, however, are useful for checking the accuracy and compatibility of data collected by other means.

U.S. Census

The 1970 Census of Population and Housing provides a summary of household statistics by census tract, and includes data on the journey to work, travel mode, income, unemployment duration, race, and age. This represents an excellent source of data, for use either directly or as a control, to check on the validity of other data sources. It should be noted that special cross tabulations may be made for data not in summary tapes.

Choosing and Operating a Transit Improvement

Technical and Legal Constraints

The choice of a transit improvement for increasing the accessibility of a low-income area should be based on a comprehensive analysis of independent alternative plans. As discussed in Chapter 7, the recommendation of a "best plan" depends heavily on the ability to prepare test plans which are well thought out. It is not so much a question of whether to favor a demand-responsive, door-to-door system versus a more conventional type of service. But rather, it is a question of which system or combination of systems produces the largest increase in accessibility.

In the case study of Chapter 7 the point was made that a door-to-door transit system was less effective than an express shuttle service. But the two systems combined proved to be the most effective solution for Brownsville. This finding, however, may be unique for New York City, where there exists a good trunk system of rapid transit facilities. In a smaller or less dense urban area, however, it may not be advantageous to recommend a similar mix of transportation improvements.

It should be noted that finding the best functional transit improvement does not necessarily imply that it *may* be implemented. As was shown in Chapter 4 for the demonstration projects which were reviewed, the new project bus routes were not permitted to operate *directly* to areas of employment, but were constrained to more *indirect* routings by the existing franchise patterns. In effect, a franchise reserves an area for the exclusive control of a transit company. There usually is no reciprocity between two adjoining franchise operations. What this means for the low-income traveler of Long Island, for example, is not only an increase in travel *time*, but also an increase in travel *cost*. Thus, in Long Island it was found that the bus transit improvements were only marginally better than the already existing service. In some cases bus fares amounted to over $2.00 per round trip per day, or over 10 percent of the daily gross wage. Thus the partial removal of the time constraint may have been offset by retaining a high fare structure which must have inhibited work opportunities. As a result the potential impact of these improvements was significantly minimized. It is incompatible to think that it is possible to improve low-skilled job accessibilities and expect that the riders of transit facilities will pay the costs of the service. Throughout the country, transit companies require subsidies to cover the difference between service cost and fare revenues. Although this is not the case for many individual transit routes which operate in very high-density transit corridors, the costs of operating those routes which feed the travel lines far exceeds their revenues; thus, on a system-wide basis, the transit industry requires public subsidy.

When one considers that the wages of the unskilled worker are the lowest of all workers, it should be obvious that his ability to pay for transportation to a job is considerably less than that of an average worker. It follows then, that the amount of subsidy required to operate a transit system serving a poverty area should exceed that provided for the average community. Whenever this condition does not exist, the attractiveness of a source of employment is greatly reduced, and the effectiveness of a physical transportation improvement will not be detected. Thus, providing a transit connection between a low-income area and an employment area is only one-half of the task; the other half requiring fares which can be afforded by the potential rider. This proposition ought to be considered especially in cases where transit improvements from the inner city to suburban jobs are advocated.

Marketing the Service

It should be noted further that projected reductions in unemployment brought about by improvements in the transportation accessibility of an area, should not be expected to materialize as soon as the improved service is in operation. During the project planning phase, and throughout the initial months of operations, vigorous marketing campaigns should be conducted in the affected areas to acquaint the potential rider and the potential employer with the newly established service.

Marketing the service through advertising the importance of the improvement; identifying areas of improved access; and explaining to the riding public how the improvements complement the existing transit system, is a necessary requirement in the achievement of the projected unemployment reduction. In addition, information about job openings should be made available *in* the vehicles and other readily accessible locations in the community.

Demand Volume Constraints

In the case study of Chapter 7, the determination of the number and type of vehicles which are required to implement the proposed alternative plans was found to depend *primarily* on the amount of travel which occurs in the corridors of improved accessibility, and *secondarily* on the demand which promulgates the plans.

It is possible, therefore, to find cases where, although the worth of a public transit improvement may be justified economically when the service is evaluated for the exclusive use of the newly employed, the presence of a large volume of *existing* travel in the corridors of improvement may *dictate* the need for additional vehicles whose cost will render the proposed improvements counter-productive. A case in which this situation may occur is illustrated in Table 9-1 which shows that the benefits, which are a fraction of the newly employed workers, are exceeded by the cost of service, which depends on the total demand volume.

Table 9-1
A Condition Where Costs May Exceed Benefits

Type of Demand	Demand Volume	Benefits	Costs
Newly employed	100	$420,000	$250,000
Existing travel	1000	–	500,000
Total	1100	420,000	750,000

Whenever such a condition would develop, the improvements could not be justified on economic grounds.

Multiple Vehicle Use

While, in this book, we have discussed the travel needs of the poor only in terms of home-to-work needs, it is usually the case that the transportation deficiencies of low-income areas are not confined to places of employment. The low rate of car ownership found in these areas renders the members of these communities entirely dependent on public transportation for their daily mobility requirements. This has been demonstrated virtually in every city where the problem has been researched.

It is possible, therefore, to use a large proportion of the vehicles and personnel acquired on the basis of the home-to-work transportation system, for nonwork purposes during off-peak hours. Additional mobility needs of poverty areas include trips to a doctor, hospital or clinic; and trips to shopping and to social/recreational areas. Many of these activities are not located in the CBD and, therefore, do not have adequate transit accessibility. Utilization of vehicles for these purposes, will aid in reducing the deficit of an exclusive home-to-work system.

The efficiency of vehicle utilization may be further realized by making available the vehicles of the home-to-work transit system for transporting persons whose taxi trips are now paid by the welfare agency or the Medicaid program.

Improving the Transportation Planning Process

The recent concern for *who* benefits from transportation improvements rather than the traditional concern of *what* is the benefit, stems from the need of viewing transportation facilities not only as *engineering systems* but as components of the *urban system.*[1] This concept requires, however, the ability of *relating* the transportation attributes to the goals of a community. It has not been easy, for example, to specify the transportation *requirements* in the achievement of goals such as:

1. An attractive environment.
2. Lower crime.
3. Improved public health.
4. Low unemployment.

This book has demonstrated, however, that it is possible to *convert* the goal of *low unemployment* for the poor into transportation system requirements. The transportation-accessibility model, therefore, contributes in the development of transportation plans which are responsive to this goal.

10 Conclusions

In this book we have illustrated and discussed the kinds and severity of problems faced by the disadvantaged when they are not provided with a transportation service which permits them to achieve a degree of mobility which is at par with that enjoyed by the nondisadvantaged population. We have discussed and evaluated the impact of inadequate transportation services on the poor, the young, the aged, and the handicapped.

We have not covered fully all the possible ramifications associated with reduced or severely limited mobility: for example, in the discussion of the poor we have concentrated primarily on the job-related aspects of mobility. We have not, however, treated equally well the need of the poor for transportation services which link them with shopping, recreation, medical, and social opportunities. Techniques for objectively analyzing these issues are yet to be developed. And we hope that the work presented in this book will motivate others to carry out complementary studies and research which will document the importance of transportation on all aspects of the mobility needs of this group.

Our discussion of the young has been centered on the issue of improving the planning criteria to provide transportation services responsive to the needs of young people. Their need for travel is perhaps most felt in the problems they find in gaining access to recreational activities and job opportunities. Much recreational land, such as beaches, state parks, ski areas, and other types of open space, has been made accessible primarily by automobile. Few opportunities exist for reaching these areas by public transportation. When they do exist they are unreasonably priced, so that the young are not able to afford these services. Hitchhiking is the only available means of travel for many of them. Yet this mode is outlawed in many states and on many toll facilities.

For the young who live in suburban and rural areas, the lack of an automobile can prevent them from holding summer jobs, or even part-time jobs while they are in school. These are the youngsters who are usually in greatest need for some income to provide additional help toward their tuition or family livelihood. Lack of public transportation services for them, therefore, imposes undue hardships by restricting job and recreational opportunities. It was noted that the local governments do not go beyond the recognition of providing transportation services for the purpose of going to school and back. However, the needs of the young go beyond this segment of life space, and, in fact, extend to their natural desire to explore the best opportunities which are available in the region which will permit the young without access to a car to reach them for maximum satisfaction of recreational, cultural, social and employment needs.

The public concern with and commitment to the provision of transportation services for the disadvantaged has perhaps been most evident with the aged. This very visible component of society is the only group which has been considered seriously by legislative bodies, in the sense that they are provided a continued subsidy of their transportation costs. The impact of this action has been manifested by an observed increase in mass transit ridership by elderly patrons on virtually all transit systems where reduced fares are in effect.

However, many elderly persons are also handicapped, or live in areas not well served by mass transit service. These individuals are not the ones who can avail themselves of the fruits of reduced fares. They require special services which are capable of transporting them from the front doors of their homes to the front doors of their desired destinations. Although several efforts have been made in various parts of the country in this regard, most of these special services have not been long-lasting, due to a lack of public funds to permit continued subsidy.

As for the last set of the disadvantaged discussed in our book, namely the handicapped, we have seen an almost complete neglect of this group by the government. They are, nevertheless, perhaps the ones in greatest need of easily accessible transportation.

Psychologically they tend to set themselves apart from the rest of society, just as much as society sets them apart. They are, however, individuals whose needs for travel are not different from those manifested by the rest of the population. Depending on the severity of the handicap, an individual has different requirements for accessible transportation. The person using a wheelchair cannot possibly use a public bus or rapid transit line unless provisions are made in the vehicle to handle a wheelchair. Similarly, someone on crutches, or who suffers from rheumatism, will find it painful negotiating an average step to get on or off a bus or to climb or descend the set of stairs leading to and from a rapid transit platform. The handicapped are, therefore, surrounded by a multitude of architectural barriers which inhibit their mobility. That there is a demand for barrier-free transit is an unavoidable conclusion. One study shows a potential increase in travel of 72 percent. Table 10-1 shows estimates of latent demand based on interviews of disadvantaged persons. These barriers, however, are not found exclusively in public transportation facilities but, in fact, are present in most man-made environments, ranging from the doorways in buildings to toilet facilities. Therefore it is not very clear that by lowering travel barriers alone there will, in effect, be produced marked improvements in the mobility of this group. Architectural barriers should also be eliminated within the infrastructure of human activities. And the removal of barriers in the transportation system should be done in combination with the removal of barriers from all man-made structures and artifacts.

A last point that needs to be made here relates to the concept that was introduced at the beginning of this book. This concerns the area of definition of who is considered to be disadvantaged in the transportation sense. We have shown, for example, that our four types of disadvantaged: the poor, the young, the aged, and the handicapped, are not mutually exclusive groups. In fact, a significant amount of overlap is found between groups. As was discussed earlier, the greater the number of subsets formed when these groups intersect (see Figure 10-1) the more severe is the degree of disadvantage experienced by individuals belonging to these subsets. The severity of this disadvantage, however, varies in accordance to the state or combination of states in which individuals may be classified.

Although commonalities exist among groups, i.e., being aged most often implies being poor; and being handicapped is a frequent characteristic of the aged, it does not necessarily follow that the *needs* for transportation for these groups are similar. For example, removing the physical barriers on transportation facilities will improve the mobility of the handicapped and the aged and the young. But the increases in mobility resulting from these improvements will differ among these groups. These differentials in travel benefits will occur because the *need for travel* of the aged is primarily manifested by their trip types, which consist of two predominant trip purposes: *medical* and *shopping* trips. But the needs for travel of the handicapped population are more intense, because they include *normal mobility desires* which do not differ from those of the average population. Thus it may be stated that, although a specific improvement may satisfy a physical requirement which is common to several groups, the impact of the improvement will be more effective for one group than for another.

It is necessary, then, to consider the specific needs of groups, of subsets of groups, and even of individuals, in planning and designing means of improving

Table 10-1
Latent Travel Demand of the Handicapped and Elderly

Trip Purpose	Current Travel (Trips/Person/Day)	Additional Travel (Trips/Person/Day)*	Potential % Increase
Work/school	0.14	0.02	14%
Shopping	0.17	0.14	82%
Medical/dental	0.12	0.06	50%
Social/recreational	0.18	0.20	111%
Church	0.13	0.11	85%
Total	0.74	0.53	72%

*Additional trips that respondents said they would take if they had access to a barrier-free system at no cost.

Source: Abt Associates Inc., *Accessibility of the Metropolitan Washington, D.C. Public Transportation System to the Handicapped and Elderly*, Cambridge, Mass., August 1972, Tables 9 and 19.

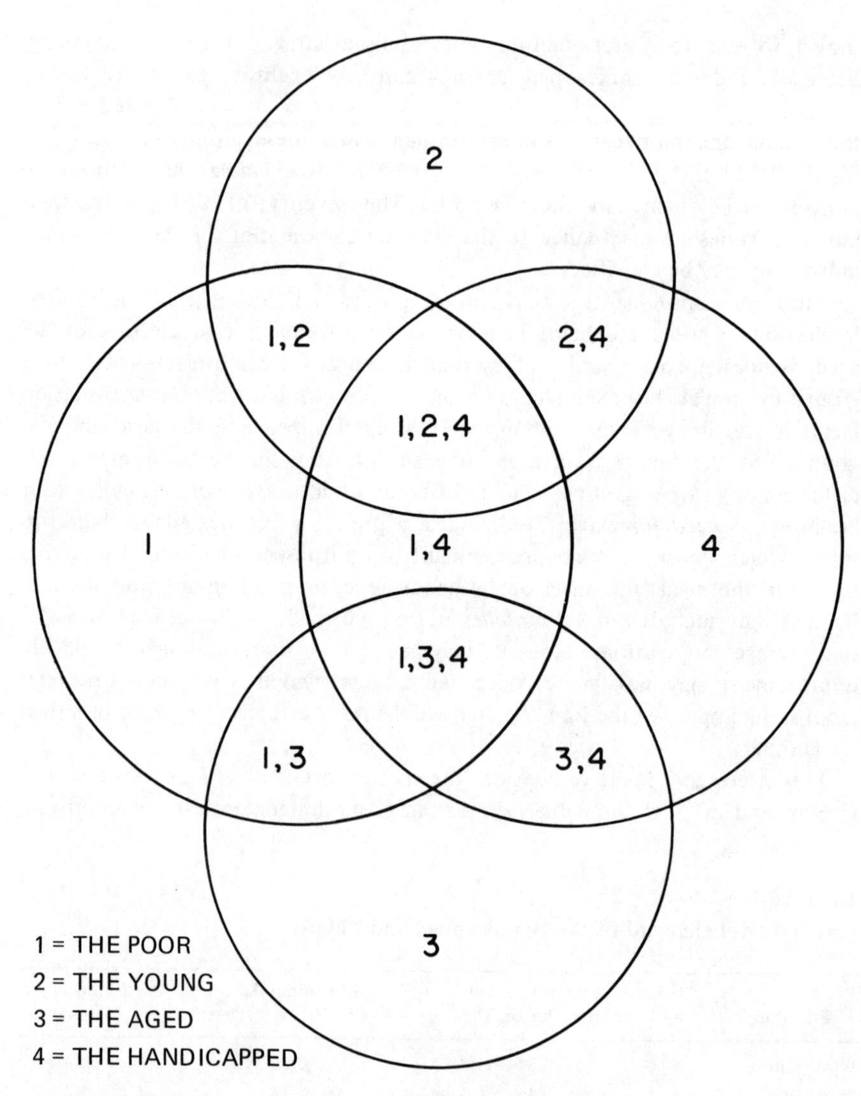

Figure 10-1. Sets and Subsets of the Transportation Disadvantaged Population

mobility. It is necessary, also, to see the improvement of personal mobility as more than a desirable quality; it is a *necessity* to the full development and quality of life of all citizens. And it is necessary, in sum, to approach the improvement of mobility from the standpoint of *universality*: the reduction of fares for one group of the poor should benefit other segments of the poor; the inauguration of new services for the elderly should point the way to new services for the handicapped and the young; and the elimination of physical barriers eases the plight not only of the old and the handicapped, but of the average citizen as well.

Appendixes

Appendix A: Unemployment Reduction

Table A-1
Existing Transit Travel Time and Travel Time Factor (F_{Aj}) from Brownsville Residential Area to Industrial Employment Zones.

Employment Zones	No. of Unskilled Jobs per Zone (E_j)	Travel Time (TT_{Aj})	Travel Time Factor (F_{Aj})
1	1630	44 min.	0.47
2	3159	50	0.40
3	2967	49	0.40
4	4605	62	0.27
5	441	43	0.48
6	1049	83	0.15
7	1849	55	0.34
8	484	62	0.27
9	7028	50	0.40
10	3960	48	0.41
11	2704	42	0.50
12	5669	47	0.42

Table A-2
Travel Time and Travel Time Factors for Door-to-Door Transit System: Maximum, Intermediate, and Minimum Alternatives

Employment Zones	Maximum		Intermediate		Minimum	
	TT_{Aj}	FA_j	TT_{Aj}	FA_j	TT_{Aj}	FA_j
1	30	0.87	30	0.87	35	0.68
2	34	0.70	39	0.57	44	0.45
3	23	1.35	45	0.45	50	0.40
4	30	0.87	30	0.87	35	0.68
5	20	1.70	20	1.70	25	1.20
6	49	0.40	54	0.35	59	0.31
7	31	0.82	31	0.82	36	0.65
8	35	0.68	40	0.55	45	0.45
9	36	0.65	45	0.45	50	0.40
10	23	1.35	23	1.35	28	0.98
11	25	1.20	35	0.68	40	0.55
12	28	0.98	43	0.49	47	0.42

Table A-3
Accessibility Changes for the Maximum Plan

Employment Zone	ΔF_{Aj} Max. = (F_{Aj} Max. Plan) – (F_{Aj} Existing Transit Ser.)	(E_j) (ΔF_{Aj} Max.)
1	0.87 – 0.47 = 0.40	653
2	0.70 – 0.40 = 0.30	946
3	1.35 – 0.40 = 0.95	2820
4	0.87 – 0.27 = 0.60	2770
5	1.70 – 0.48 = 1.22	539
6	0.40 – 0.15 = 0.25	262
7	0.82 – 0.34 = 0.48	887
8	0.68 – 0.27 = 0.41	198
9	0.65 – 0.40 = 0.25	1760
10	1.35 – 0.41 = 0.94	3450
11	1.20 – 0.50 = 0.70	1890
12	0.98 – 0.42 = 0.56	3180
	E_j (ΔF_{Aj} max.) =	19,355

Reduction in Unemployment for Maximum Plan = $Y_{Max.}$

X_A (Max. Plan) = 180,000 + 19,355 = 199,355
∴ ΔY_A (Max.) = 31.65 (log 199,355 – log 18,000) = 1.58%

Table A-4
Accessibility Changes for the Intermediate Plan

Employment Zone	ΔF_{Aj} Int. = (F_{Aj} Int. Plan) – (F_{Aj} Existing Transit Ser.)	(E_j) (ΔF_{Aj} Int.)
1	0.87 – 0.47 = 0.40	653
2	0.57 – 0.40 = 0.17	537
3	0.45 – 0.40 = 0.05	148
4	0.87 – 0.27 = 0.60	2770
5	1.70 – 0.48 = 1.22	539
6	0.35 – 0.15 = 0.20	210
7	0.82 – 0.34 = 0.48	887
8	0.55 – 0.27 = 0.28	136
9	0.45 – 0.40 = 0.05	350
10	1.35 – 0.41 = 0.94	3450
11	0.68 – 0.50 = 0.18	486
12	0.49 – 0.42 = 0.07	398
	(E_j) (ΔF_{Aj} Int) =	10,564

Reduction in Unemployment for Intermediate Plan = $Y_{Int.}$

X_A (Intermediate Plan) = 18,000 + 10,564 = 190,564
ΔY_A (Int.) = 31.65 (log 190,564 – log 180,000) = 0.95%

Table A-5
Accessibility Changes for the Minimum Plan

Employment Zone	ΔF_{Aj} Min. = (F_{Aj} Min. Plan) – (F_{Aj} Existing Transit Ser.)	(E_j) (ΔF_{Aj} Min.)
1	0.68 – 0.47 = 0.21	342
2	0.45 – 0.40 = 0.05	158
3	0.40 – 0.40 = 0	158
4	0.68 – 0.27 = 0.41	1890
5	1.20 – 0.48 = 0.72	318
6	0.31 – 0.15 = 0.16	168
7	0.65 – 0.34 = 0.31	560
8	0.45 – 0.27 = 0.18	87
9	0.40 – 0.40 = 0	–
10	0.98 – 0.41 = 0.57	2260
11	0.55 – 0.50 = 0.05	135
12	0.42 – 0.42 = 0	–
	E_j ($\Delta F_{Aj\ \text{min.}}$) =	5,918
	Reduction in Unemployment for Minimum Plan = $Y_{\text{Min.}}$	

X_A (Min. Plan) = 180,000 + 5,918 = 185,918

$\therefore \Delta Y_A$ (Min.) = 31.65 (log 185,918 – log 180,000) = 0.63%

Appendix B: Distribution of Work Trips and Cost Estimates for Proposed Door-to-Door Alternative Plans

Table B-1
Work Trip Destinations of the Newly Employed Using the Maximum Plan

Work Trip Distribution Estimates with the Gravity Model

$$T_{Aj} = T_A \times \frac{E_j F_{Aj}}{\sum_{1}^{12} E_j F_{Aj}} \quad ; \; T_A = 162$$

Destination Employment Zone	E_j	F_{Aj}	$E_j F_{Aj}$	$\frac{E_j F_{Aj}}{\Sigma E_j F_{Aj}}$	T_{Aj}
1	1630	0.87	1420	0.04	6
2	3159	0.70	2210	0.07	11
3	2967	1.35	4000	0.12	19
4	4605	0.87	4000	0.12	19
5	441	1.70	750	0.02	3
6	1049	0.40	420	0.01	2
7	1809	0.82	1480	0.04	7
8	484	0.68	330	0.01	2
9	7028	0.65	4560	0.14	23
10	3960	1.35	5350	0.16	26
11	2704	1.20	3250	0.10	16
12	5669	0.98	5560	0.17	28
			Σ = 33,030	1.00	162

Table B-2
Work Trip Destinations of the Newly Employed Using the Intermediate Plan

$$T_{Aj} = T_A \times \frac{E_jF_{Aj}}{\sum_{1}^{12} E_jF_{Aj}} \; ; \; T_A = 97$$

Destination Employment Zones	E_j	F_{Aj}	E_jF_{Aj}	$\frac{E_jF_{Aj}}{\Sigma E_jF_{Aj}}$	T_{Aj}
1	1630	0.87	1420	0.06	6
2	3159	0.57	1800	0.07	7
3	2967	0.45	1340	0.05	5
4	4605	0.87	4000	0.16	16
5	441	1.70	750	0.03	3
6	1049	0.35	370	0.02	2
7	1809	0.82	1480	0.06	6
8	484	0.55	270	0.01	–
9	7028	0.45	3160	0.13	13
10	3460	1.35	5350	0.22	21
11	2704	0.68	1840	0.07	7
12	5669	0.49	2780	0.12	11
			Σ = 24,560	1.00	97

Table B-3
Work Trip Destinations of the Newly Employed Using the Minimum Plan

$$T_{Aj} = T_A \times \frac{E_j F_{Aj}}{\sum_{1}^{12} E_j F_{Aj}} \; ; \; T_A = 66$$

Destination Employment Zones	E_j	F_{Aj}	$E_j F_{Aj}$	$\frac{E_j F_{Aj}}{\Sigma E_j F_{Aj}}$	T_{Aj}
1	1630	0.68	1108	0.06	4
2	3159	0.45	1422	0.07	5
3	2967	0.40	1187	0.06	4
4	4605	0.68	3131	0.16	10
5	441	1.20	529	0.03	2
6	1049	0.31	325	0.02	1
7	1809	0.65	1176	0.06	4
8	484	0.45	218	0.01	1
9	7028	0.40	2811	0.14	9
10	3960	0.98	3881	0.20	13
11	2704	0.55	1487	0.07	5
12	5669	0.42	2381	0.12	8
			Σ = 19,656	1.00	66

Table B-4
Origin-Destination of the Newly Employed–The Maximum Plan

Brownsville Subareas of Origin	Employment Zones of Destination												
	1	2	3	4	5	6	7	8	9	10	11	12	Total
a	2	4	6	6	1	1	2	1	8	9	5	9	54
b	2	4	6	6	1	1	2	1	8	9	5	9	54
c	2	4	6	6	1	1	2	1	8	9	5	9	54
Total	6	12	18	18	3	3	6	3	24	27	15	27	162

Table B-5
Origin-Destination of the Newly Employed–The Intermediate Plan

Brownsville Subareas of Origin	Employment Zones of Destination					
	Route I 1-2-3	Route II 4	Route III 5-6	Route IV 7-8-9	Route V 10-11-12	Total
a	7	5	2	6	13	33
b	6	5	2	6	13	32
c	6	5	2	6	13	32
Total	19	15	6	18	39	97

Table B-6
Origin-Destination of the Newly Employed–The Minimum Plan

Brownsville Subareas of Origin	Employment Zones of Destination: Route I 1-2-3	Route II 4	Route III 5-6	Route IV 7-8-9	Route V 10-11-12	Total
a,b,c (combined)	13	10	3	14	26	66

Table B-7
Existing Work Trips between Brownsville and Employment Zones

Employment Zones	No. of Brownsville Workers Currently Employed
1	18
2	34
3	23
4	18
5	4
6	7
7	6
8	–
9	16
10	45
11	21
12	20
Total	212

Table B-8
Total Demand on the Maximum Plan: Existing Travel Added to Forcast Trips

Subareas of Origin	Employment Zones of Destination: 1	2	3	4	5	6	7	8	9	10	11	12
a	8	15	14	12	2	3	4	1	13	24	12	16
b	8	15	14	12	2	3	4	1	13	24	12	16
c	8	15	14	12	2	3	4	1	13	24	12	16
Total	24	45	42	36	6	9	12	3	39	72	36	48
Type of Vehicle	Van	Van	Van	Van	Auto	Auto	Auto	Auto	Van	Minibus	Van	Minibus

Table B-9
Total Demand on the Intermediate Plan

	Employment Zones of Destination				
Subareas of Origin	Route I 1-2-3	Route II 4	Route III 5-6	Route IV 7-8-9	Route V 10-11-12
a	32	11	5	13	42
b	31	11	5	13	42
c	31	11	5	13	42
Total	94	33	15	39	126
Type of Vehicle	Medium Bus	Econoline	Auto	Econoline	Standard Bus

Table B-10
Total Demand on the Minimum Plan

	Employment Zones of Destination				
Subareas of Origin	Route I 1-2-3	Route II 4	Route III 5-6	Route IV 7-8-9	Route V 10-11-12
a,b,c (combined)	88	28	14	36	112
Vehicle Type	Medium Bus	Medium Bus	Econoline	Medium Bus	Medium Buses

I. Cost Estimate of Maximum Plan

1. Vehicle Requirements
   - Automobiles: 3 x 4 = 12
   - Ford Econoline Vans: 3 x 6 = 18
   - Minibuses: 3 x 2 = 6
2. Vehicle Costs (Including cost of communication equipment @ $500/radio)

   Automobiles: 12 x $4,000 = $ 48,000
   Vans: 18 x $6,500 = 117,000
   Minibuses: 6 x 20,500 = 123,000
   $288,000

   CRF (for 5-year life @ i = 8%) = 0.25
3. Annual Capital Cost of Vehicles = 0.25 x $288,000 = $72,000
4. Annual Salary for *39 Drivers*: 39 x 52 wks. x $200/wk = $405,000

5. Cost of Maintenance, Gas, Oil, Tires @ \$0.12/mile
   Ave. miles driven per day = 16 x 36 vehicles = 576 veh.-miles
   Yearly: 576 x 250 days = 144,000 veh.-miles x 0.12 = \$17,280
6. Insurance @ \$1,000/vehicle = \$36,000
7. Dispatcher = \$10,000
8. Office and Garage Rental @ 300 S.F./veh. x 36 vehicles = 10,800 S.F.
   10,800 x \$3.00/S.F. = \$32,400
9. Telephone, Utilities, Bookkeeping, etc. = \$5,000

Summary of Costs

1. Vehicles	=	\$ 72,000
2. Drivers	=	405,600
3. Maintenance	=	17,280
4. Insurance	=	36,000
5. Dispatcher	=	10,000
6. Office & Garage Rental	=	32,400
7. Office Expenses	=	5,000
Total Costs		\$578,280

10. "Net" Revenues (Excluding revenues of riders who switched):
    \$0.70/worker/day
    0.70 x 162 workers x 250 days = \$28,350
11. Net Cost of Service = 578,280 – 28,350 = \$549,930

II. Cost Estimate of Intermediate Plan

1. Vehicle Requirements:

Automobiles:	3 x 1 = 3
Econoline Vans:	3 x 2 = 6
Medium Buses:	3 x 1 = 3
Standard Buses:	3 x 1 = 3

2. Vehicle Costs (Including Cost of Communication Equipment @ \$500/radio)

Automobiles:	3 x \$4,000 =	\$ 12,000
Vans:	6 x 6,500 =	39,000
Medium Buses:	3 x 30,000 =	90,000
Standard Buses:	3 x 40,000 =	120,000
		\$261,000

CRF (for 5 year life @ i = 8%) = 0.25

3. Annual Capital Cost of Vehicles: 0.25 x 261,000 = $65,250
4. Maintenance: 16 miles/vehicle x 15 vehicles = 240 miles/day
   240 x 250 days = 60,000 vehicle miles
   @ $0.15/vehicle = $9,000
5. Insurance @ $1,000/vehicle = $15,000
6. Dispatcher = $10,000
7. Office and Garage Rental @ 400 S.F./veh. x 15 veh. = 6,000 S.F.
   @ $3.00/S.F. = $18,000
8. Annual Salary for 16.25 drivers: 16.25 x 52 wks. x $200/wk = $169,000
9. Telephone, Utilities, Bookkeeping = $5,000

Summary of Costs

1. Vehicles	= $ 65,250
2. Drivers	= 169,000
3. Maintenance	= 9,000
4. Insurance	= 15,000
5. Dispatcher	= 10,000
6. Office & Garage Rental	= 18,000
7. Office Expenses	= 5,000
Total Costs	$291,250

10. Net Revenues (Excluding revenues of riders who switched)
    $0.70/worker/day
    0.70 x 97 workers x 250 days = $16,975
11. Net Cost of Service = $291,250 – 16,975 = $274,275

III. Cost Estimate of Minimum Plan

1. Vehicle Requirements:

Ford Econoline Van	= 1
Medium Buses	= 8

2. Vehicle Costs (Including Cost of Communication Equipment @ $500/radio)

Van:	1 x 6,500 = $ 6,500
Medium Buses:	8 x 30,000 = 240,000
	$246,500

   CRF (for 5 year life @ i = 8%) = 0.25
3. Annual Capital Cost of Vehicles: 0.25 x 246,500 = $61,625

4. Annual Salary for 9.75 drivers: 9.75 x 52 wks. x $200/wk = $101,400
5. Maintenance: 16 miles x 9 vehicles = 144 veh.miles/day
   144 x 250 = 36,000 veh.miles
   @ $0.15/veh.mile = $5,400
6. Insurance @ $1,000/vehicle = $9,000
7. Dispatcher = $10,000
8. Office and Garage Rental @ 400 S.F./veh. = 3,600 S.F.
   @ $3.00/S.F. = $10,800
9. Telephone, Utilities, Bookkeeping = $5,000

Summary of Costs

1. Vehicles	=	$ 61,625
2. Drivers	=	101,400
3. Maintenance	=	5,400
4. Insurance	=	9,000
5. Dispatcher	=	10,000
6. Office & Garage Rental	=	10,800
7. Office Expenses	=	5,000
Total Costs		$204,225

10. Net Revenues (Excluding revenues of riders who switched)
    @ $0.70/worker/day
    0.70 x 65 workers x 250 days = $11,375
11. Net Costs = $204,225 – 11,375 = $192,850

Appendix C: Shuttle Express Service to Transportation Centroid

Estimate of Unemployment Reduction for the Shuttle Express to Transportation Centroid

The number of jobs reached from Brownsville via the transportation centroid, at specific travel time intervals is calculated below:

1. The travel time to the transportation centroid via the Express Shuttle is 12 minutes (4 min. access time + 8 min. riding time).
2. Refer to Table A-1.
3. The number of jobs reached in 30 min. from Brownsville equals the number of jobs reached in 18 min. (30-12) of travel time from the transportation centroid. So that:
   For 30 min. from Brownsville, enter 18 min. in Fig. A
   For 45 min. from Brownsville, enter 33 min. in Fig. A
   For 60 min. from Brownsville, enter 48 min. in Fig. A

   Next:

	No. of Jobs	ΔJobs	ΔF_{Aj}	for Range
@18 min.	29,000	29,000	2.30	0-30 min.
@33 min.	115,000	86,000	0.64	30-45 min.
@48 min.	393,000	287,000	0.36	45-60 min.

4. Calculation of new accessibility index for Brownsville:
   $X_{At} = 2.30(29{,}000) + 0.64(86{,}000) + 0.36(278{,}000) = 221{,}700$
   $\log_{10} 221{,}700 = 5.344$

   $\therefore Y_A = 186.26 - 31.65(5.344) = 16.25\%$

   $Y_A = 19.60 - 16.25 = 3.35\%$

Appendix D: Vehicle Requirements and Costs for the Express Shuttle Service

I. Shuttle Express Travel Demand and Vehicle Supply from Brownsville to Transportation Centroid

Forecast Trips	= 334
Existing Trips	= 2700
Total Demand	= 3034

Assume that demand for service is from 7:30 to 8:30 A.M.; then, re-use factor is
Re-use Factor = 60 min. ÷ 24 min. per round trip
= 2.5 trips per bus
No. of Bus Trips per hour = 3034 ÷ 50 persons/bus = 60
∴ 60 bus loads must be produced in one hour.
This requires 60 ÷ 2.5 = 16 Standard Buses.

II. Cost Estimate of Shuttle Express Service

1. Vehicle Requirements: 16 Standard Buses
2. Vehicle Costs: 16 x 40,000 = $650,000; CRF (5 Yr. Life, $i = 8\%$) =0.25
3. Annual Capital Cost of Vehicles: 0.25 x 640,000 = $160,000
4. Annual Salary for 17.33 drivers: 17.33 x 52 wks. x $200/week = 180,232.
5. Maintenance: 144 veh. miles/day x 250 days = 36,000 veh. miles @ $0.20/veh.mile = $7,200.
6. Insurance @ $1,000/veh. = $16,000.
7. Office and Garage Rental @ 400 sf/Veh. x 16 vehicles = 6400 SF @ $3.00/SF = $19,200.
8. Manager/Dispatcher = $12,000.
9. Telephone & Utilities, Bookkeeper = $5,000.

a)	Vehicles	=	$160,000
b)	Drivers	=	180,200
c)	Maintenance	=	7,200
d)	Insurance	=	16,000
e)	Space Rented	=	19,200
f)	Manager/Dispatcher	=	12,000
g)	Office Expenses	=	5,000
	Total Costs	=	$399,600

10. Revenues lost by other transit lines

    1500 x \$0.70/day = \$1050/day

    Annual Loss = 1050 x 250 = \$262,500

    Since the Express Shuttle is free, this amount is a net loss.

∴ Real Total Cost = \$399,600

262,500

\$662,100

Notes

Notes

Chapter 1
Background

1. *1972 New York Times Almanac*, The New York Times, New York, N.Y. 1972.

2. *Manpower Report of the President*, U.S. Department of Labor, transmitted to Congress, April 1971.

3. Ibid.

4. *Conference on Transportation and Human Needs in the 70's: The Second Phase* (Proceedings), The American University, Washington, D.C., 1972.

5. "Characteristics of the Low-Income Population: 1972," in *Consumer Income*, U.S. Department of Commerce Series P-60, No. 88, Washington, D.C., June 1973.

6. Lassow, W., "The Effect of the Fare Increase of July 1966 on the Number of Passengers Carried on the New York City Transit System," *Highway Research Board*, Record No. 213, Washington, D.C., 1968.

7. *Violence in the City–An End or a Beginning?*, Governor's Commission on the Los Angeles Riots, Los Angeles, Calif., 1965.

8. Ibid.

9. *Transportation Requirements and Characteristics of Low-Income Families as Related to Job Availability in Non-CBD Employment Concentrations*, Final Report to the Tri-State Transportation Commission, Polytechnic Institute of Brooklyn, December 30, 1968.

10. For example, see: (a) Paaswell, Robert E., et al., "The Mobility of Inner City Residents," a study for Buffalo, N.Y., Department of Civil Engineering, State University of New York at Buffalo; (b) *Transportation Between Poverty Pockets and Employment Centers*, Planning Department, City of Worcester, Mass., 1969; (c) *Getting to Work from West Oakland: Problems and Solutions*, an analysis of transportation problems in West Oakland and four complementary proposals for their solutions, City Planning Department, Oakland, Calif., 1970; (d) *Denver Home to Work Transportation Study*, a study of the transportation problems faced by residents of Denver's poverty neighborhoods, Alan M. Voorhees and Associates, 1969; (e) *Transportation Accessibility from the Nashville Model Cities Area*, Nashville, Tenn., Alan M. Voorhees and Associates, 1969.

11. Ornati, Oscar A., *Transportation Needs of the Poor,* Praeger Publishers, New York, 1969.

12. Floyd, Thomas H., Jr., "Using Transportation to Alleviate Poverty: A Progress Report on Experiments Under the Mass Transportation Act," paper presented at the Conference on Poverty and Transportation, American Academy of Arts and Sciences, Brookline, Mass., June 7, 1968, Table 2.

13. Ibid., p. 9.

14. Pignataro, Louis J., and Falcocchio, John C., "Transportation Needs of Low-Income Families," *Traffic Quarterly*, October 1969.

15. *President's Message to Congress on Civil Rights*, April 28, 1966.

16. *Conference on Transportation and Human Needs in the 70's.*

17. *Manpower Report of the President.*

18. Ibid.

19. Ibid.

20. Ibid.

21. *Violence in the City.*

22. *Conference on Transportation and Human Needs in the 70's.*

23. *The Handicapped and Elderly Market for Urban Mass Transit*, Transportation Systems Center, NTIS PB 224821, Department of Transportation, Cambridge, Mass., October 1973.

24. Ibid.

25. *Conference on Transportation and Human Needs in the 70's.*

26. *The Handicapped and Elderly Market for Urban Mass Transit.*

27. Ibid.

Chapter 2
Some Basic Concepts

1. Orski, C.D., "The Urban Transportation Planning Process: In Search of Improved Strategy," *Highway Research Board*, Record No. 309, Washington, D.C., 1970.

2. For example, see *Chicago Area Transportation Study*, Volumes 1, 2, 3, 1959-1962, Chicago, Ill.; and *1985 Regional Projections for the Delaware Valley*, Delaware Valley Regional Planning Commission, Philadelphia, Pa., 1967.

3. Voorhees, A.M., and Bellomo, S.J., "Urban Travel and City Structure," *Highway Research Board*, Record No. 322, Washington, D.C., 1970.

4. Wohl, Martin, "Must Something be Done About Traffic Congestion?," *Traffic Quarterly*, July 1971.

5. Wickstrom, George V., "Defining Balanced Transportation—A Question of Opportunity," *Traffic Quarterly*, July 1971.

6. Murphy, Robert H., "The Boston Transportation Review, A Re-Evaluation of Expressway's Values in an Urban Area," *Traffic Engineering*, June 1971.

7. For example, see: (a) Bellomo, S.J., and Provost, S.C., "Toward an Evaluation of Subarea Transportation Systems," *Highway Research Board*, Record No. 293, Washington, D.C., 1969; (b) Voorhees, A.M., "Current Techniques to Shape the Urban Form," *Highway Research Board*, Record No. 137, Washington, D.C., 1966; (c) Manheim, M.L., "Principles of Transport Systems

Analysis," *Highway Research Board*, Record No. 180, Washington, D.C., 1967; (c) Kochanowski, R. and Wickstrom, G.V., "On Improving the Transportation Planning Process," *Highway Research Board*, Record No. 309, Washington, D.C., 1970.

8. *A Statement on National Transportation Policy*, U.S. Department of Transportation, 1971.

Chapter 3
A Review of the Issues

1. *The New York Times*, May 30, 1971.

2. *Automobile Facts and Figures*, The Automobile Manufacturers Association, 1971.

3. Bone, A.J., and Wohl, Martin, "Massachusetts Route 128 Impact Study," *Highway Research Board*, Bulletin No. 227, Washington, D.C., 1959.

4. *Tomorrow's Transportation: New Systems for the Future,* U.S. Department of Housing and Urban Development, Office of Metropolitan Development, Urban Transportation Administration, Washington, D.C., 1968.

5. *Manpower Report to the President*, U.S. Department of Labor, transmitted to Congress, April 1971, p. 89.

6. Ibid., p. 90.

7. *Tomorrow's Transportation.*

8. *Factors and Trends in Trip Lengths*, National Cooperative Highway Research Project No. 48, Washington, D.C., 1968.

9. *Tomorrow's Transportation.*

10. *Transportation Needs of Residents–Central Brooklyn Model Cities Area*, Final Report to the New York Model Cities Administration, Polytechnic Institute of Brooklyn, Department of Transportation Planning and Engineering, 1971.

11. *Special Report on Household Ownership and Purchase of Automobiles and Selected Household Durables*, U.S. Department of Commerce.

12. Myers, Sumner, "Personal Transportation for the Poor," paper presented at the Conference on Poverty and Transportation, American Academy of Arts and Sciences, Brookline, Mass., June 7, 1968.

13. *Transportation Needs of Residents*, p. 142.

14. Cantilli, E.J., and Shmelzer, J.L. (eds.), *Transportation and Aging–Selected Issues,* proceedings of the Interdisciplinary Workshop on Transportation and Aging, Department of Health, Education, and Welfare, Washington, D.C., 1970.

15. *Transportation Employment Project–South Central Los Angeles*, Final Interim Report, State of California Business and Transportation Agency, 1970.

16. *Transportation Needs of Residents.*

17. Falcocchio, J., Pignataro, L., and Cantilli, E., "Modal Choices and Travel Attributes of the Inner City Poor," *Highway Research Board*, Record No. 403, Washington, D.C., 1972.

18. Alice E. Kidder, "Transportation Policy and the Delivery of Social Services: A Small City Case Study," paper presented at the 53rd Annual Meeting of the Highway Research Board, Washington, D.C., 1974.

Chapter 4
A Review of Some Demonstration Projects

1. *Transportation Employment Project–South Central Los Angeles*, Final Interim Report, State of California Business and Transportation Agency, 1970.

2. *Automobile Facts and Figures*, The Automobile Manufacturers Association, 1971.

3. *Transportation Employment Project.*

4. *Transportation Requirements and Characteristics of Low-Income Families as Related to Job Availability in Non-CBD Employment Concentrations*, Final Report to the Tri-State Transportation Commission, Polytechnic Institute of Brooklyn, December 30, 1968.

5. Ibid.

6. Dodson, E.N., "Employment Accessibility for Special Urban Groups," General Research Corporation, System Analysis for Urban Transportation, Vol. 4, U.S. Department of Commerce, 1968.

7. *Conference on Transportation and Human Needs in the 70's: The Second Phase* (Proceedings), The American University, Washington, D.C., 1972.

8. Cantor, M.H., "The Reduced Fare Program for Older New Yorkers," in Cantilli, E.J., and Shmelzer, J.L. (eds.), *Transportation and Aging–Selected Issues*, proceedings of the Interdisciplinary Workshop on Transportation and Aging, U.S. Department of Health, Education, and Welfare, Washington, D.C., 1970.

9. Ahrens, R.J., "Reduced Fares for Senior Citizens," City of Chicago, Department of Human Resources, Division of Senior Citizens, 1970.

10. *Developments in Aging 1969*, U.S. Senate Report No. 91-875, Washington, D.C., May 1970.

11. Bell, J.H., "Senior Citizens Mobile Service," in Cantilli, Shmelzer, *Transportation and Aging.*

12. Zahora, A., "Cape May's Transportation Demonstration Project," in Cantilli and Shmelzer, ibid.

13. Crain, J., "The Minibus Brings Sparkle to Little House," in Cantilli and Shmelzer, ibid.

14. *Developments in Aging 1972*, U.S. Senate Report No. 93-147, Washington, D.C., May 1973.

15. *Conference on Transportation and Human Needs in the 70's.*
16. Ibid.
17. Ibid.
18. Ibid.
19. Ibid.
20. Ibid.
21. Rinaldi, A.T. (author), Cantilli, E.J. (editor), *Escort Service–A Final Report*, final report on the Aid to Senior Citizens Mobility in East Orange, New Jersey project, funded by the Department of Health, Education and Welfare to the Essex County Section, National Council of Jewish Women, Millburn, N.J., 1973.
22. "Final Report, Bronx, N.Y., Dial-A-Ride," Office of the Mayor, Office on Aging, New York City, 1974 (unpublished).
23. Burkhardt, J.E., letter to Dr. L.J. Pignataro, re: cost of Raleigh County Project, August 10, 1970.
24. Burkhardt, J.E., "Transportation and the Rural Elderly," in Cantilli and Shmelzer, *Transportation and Aging.*
25. Bell, "Senior Citizens Mobile Service."
26. Zahora, "Cape May's Transportation Demonstration Project."
27. Crain, "The Minibus Brings Sparkle to Little House."
28. Medville, D.M., "Dial-A-Ride Demonstration in Haddonfield: Planning and Initial Operation," in *Demand-Responsive Transportation Systems*, Special Report 136, Highway Research Board, Washington, D.C., 1973.
29. Bonsall, J.A., "Dial-A-Bus Experiment in Bay Ridges," in ibid.
30. Aex, R.P., "B-Line Dial-A-Bus System in Batavia," in ibid.
31. Oxley, P.R., "Dial-A-Ride Application in Great Britain," in ibid.
32. Roos, D., "Doorstep Transit," in *Environment*, June 1944.
33. Rinaldi and Cantilli, *Escort Service–A Final Report.*
34. "Final Report, Bronx, N.Y., Dial-A-Ride."
35. Burkhardt, "Transportation and the Rural Elderly."

Chapter 5
Improving Employment Opportunities

1. *Manpower Report to the President*, U.S. Department of Labor, transmitted to Congress, April 1971.
2. Ibid.
3. Lowrie, J.W., "Making it–The Hardest Way," *Psychology Today* 3(6), 1969, pp. 29-31, 60.
4. Morgan, Brian S., "Chronic Unemployment–Psychological versus Institutional Approaches," *Urban and Social Chance Review* 4 (1), Fall 1970.
5. *Jobs Now*, Chicago YMCA, Chicago Urban League, Illinois State Employ-

ment Service, Report No. 3, 1967. Abstracted in *Manpower Research: Inventory for Fiscal Years 1966 and 1967*, U.S. Department of Health, Education and Welfare, 1968.

6. Shrank, Robert and Stein, Susan, "Industry in the Black Community: IBM in Bedford Stuyvesant," *AIP Journal*, September 1969.

7. Ibid., p. 8.

8. Ibid.

9. Bedrosian, Hrach and Diamond, Daniel E., "Hiring Standards and Job Performance," *Manpower Research Monograph No. 18*, U.S. Department of Labor, Manpower Administration, 1970.

10. For example, see *The New York Times* March 22, March 29, 1970; August 26, September 9, 1971; and *The Wall Street Journal*, February 27, 1970.

11. Moynihan, Daniel P., *Maximum Feasible Misunderstandings: Community Action in the War on Poverty*, Free Press, New York, 1969.

12. Bernstein, Blanche, "Welfare, Work and Ambiance," *The Wall Street Journal*, February 27, 1970.

13. Durbin, Elizabeth F., *Welfare Income and Employment: An Economic Analysis of Family Choices*, Praeger Publishers, New York, 1969.

14. *Industry in the Black Community.*

15. Durbin, *Welfare Income and Employment.*

16. Bernstein, B., "Welfare, Work and Ambiance," *The Wall Street Journal*, February 27, 1970.

17. *Automobile Facts and Figures*, The Automobile Manufacturers Association, 1971.

18. For example, see the "Intervening Opportunity Model of Trip Distribution," *Chicago Area Transportation Study*, Vol. 2, Chicago, Ill., 1960, pp. 81-85.

19. Voorhees, Alan M., "A General Theory of Traffic Movement," *Proceedings*, Institute of Traffic Engineers, 1955, pp. 46-56.

20. Myers, Sumner, "Personal Transportation for the Poor," *Traffic Quarterly*, April 1970.

21. Durbin, *Welfare Income and Employment.*

22. *Transportation Requirements and Characteristics of Low-Income Families as Related to Job Availability in Non-CBD Employment Concentrations*, Final Report to the Tri-State Transportation Commission, Polytechnic Institute of Brooklyn, December 30, 1968.

23. *Transportation Needs of Residents–Central Brooklyn Model Cities Area*, Final Report to the New York City Model Cities Administration, Polytechnic Institute of Brooklyn, Department of Transportation Planning and Engineering, 1971.

Chapter 6
Improving Mobility for the Young, the Aged, and the Handicapped

1. Gelwicks, L.E., "The Older Person's Relation with the Environment: The Influence of Transportation," in Cantilli, E.J., and Shmelzer, J.L. (eds.),

Transportation and Aging–Selected Issues, proceedings of the Interdisciplinary Workshop on Transportation and Aging, Department of Health, Education, and Welfare, Washington, D.C., 1970.

2. Lewin, K., *Principles of Topological Psychology*, McGraw-Hill, New York, 1936.

3. Bach, K.W., and Gergen, K.F., "Cognitive Motivational Factors in Aging and Disengagement," in Simpson and McKenney (eds.), *Social Aspects of Aging*, Duke University Press, 1966.

4. "Characteristics of the Low-Income Population: 1972," in *Consumer Income*, U.S. Department of Commerce Series P-60, No. 88, June 1973.

5. Gelwicks, "The Older Person's Relation With The Environment."

6. Ibid.

7. *Developments in Aging 1969*, U.S. Senate Report No. 91-875, Washington, D.C., May 1970.

8. Roess, R.P., "Existing Technology in Mass Transportation," in Cantilli and Shmelzer, *Transportation and Aging.*

9. Perry, H., "The Kansas City Multi-Service Transportation (MUST) Program," in ibid.

10. Fruin, J.J., *Pedestrian Planning and Design*, MAUDEP Press, New York, 1971.

11. *The Handicapped and Elderly Market for Urban Mass Transit*, Transportation Systems Center, NTIS PB 224821, Department of Transportation, Cambridge, Mass., October 1973.

12. Ibid.

Chapter 7
Case Study: Can We Really Reduce Unemployment Through Transportation?

1. *Transportation Needs of Residents–Central Brooklyn Model Cities Area*, Final Report to the New York Model Cities Administration, Polytechnic Institute of Brooklyn, Department of Transportation Planning and Engineering, 1971.

2. Lee, B., Falcocchio, J.E., and Cantilli, E.J., "Taxicab Usage in New York City's Poverty Areas," *Highway Research Board*, Record No. 403, Washington, D.C., 1972.

Chapter 8
Discussion: Can We Really Improve The Mobility of The Disadvantaged?

1. Crain, J.L., "The Transportation Problem of Transit Dependent Persons–A Status Report," paper presented at Conference on Transportation and Human Needs, Washington, D.C., 1973.

2. Robinson, J., and Shaver, P., "Measures of Social Psychological Attitudes," Appendix B of *Measures of Political Attitudes*, Survey Research Center, Institute for Social Research, University of Michigan, Ann Arbor, Mich., 1969.

3. Thursz, D., *Where Are They Now? A Study of the Impact of Relocation on Former Residents of Southwest Washington,* Health and Welfare Council of the National Capital Area, November 1966.

4. Fellmann, G., "Sociological Field Work is Essential in Studying Community Valves," *Highway Research Board,* Record No. 305, Washington, D.C., 1970.

5. Stokols, D., "A Social-Psychological Model of Human Crowding Phenomena," *Journal of American Institute of Planners* 38(2), March 1972.

6. Colony, D., "A Study of the Impact Upon Households of Relocation from a Highway Point of View," paper presented at the 51st Annual Meeting of the Highway Research Board, Washington, D.C., 1972.

7. Willson, Harold L., "The Elderly and Handicapped on the San Francisco Bay Area Rapid System," in Cantilli, E.J., and Shmelzer, J.L. (eds.), *Transportation and Aging–Selected Issues*, proceedings of the Interdisciplinary Workshop on Transportation and Aging, Department of Health, Education, and Welfare, Washington, D.C., 1970.

Chapter 9
Unemployment and Transportation

1. *Study in New Systems of Urban Transportation*, General Motors Research Laboratories, prepared for the U.S. Department of Housing and Urban Development, February 1968.

Index

Index

About the Authors

John C. Falcocchio is Associate Professor of Transportation Planning and Engineering at the Polytechnic Institute of New York (formerly the Polytechnic Institute of Brooklyn). Prior to joining the faculty at the Polytechnic Institute, Dr. Falcocchio was a practicing transportation planner and engineer with private and public organizations. He is a professional engineer registered in New York and Pennsylvania and is an active member of several professional societies. Dr. Falcocchio has published extensively in the areas of transportation planning and transportation for the disadvantaged.

Edmund J. Cantilli is Associate Professor of Transportation Planning at the Polytechnic Institute of New York; he joined the faculty after many years as a practicing planner and engineer with the Port Authority of New York-New Jersey. He has directed and participated in research projects in many aspects of transportation, including environmental effects, transportation for the disadvantaged, and various traffic-congestion and safety problems. Dr. Cantilli is active as a professional consultant and as a member of planning and engineering professional societies. He is the author or editor of numerous articles and books, including *Programming Environmental Improvements in Public Transportation* (Lexington Books, 1974).